WHAT TO EXPECT FROM
◀THE DISTRACTED YOGI

Have you ever experienced the longing to be fully-understood or fully-appreciated?

Then,

Discovered that you no-longer understand yourself anymore so how could you possibly hope for anyone else to 'Get' You?

Then,

You are someone who will love & appreciate the true story that is The Distracted Yogi.

& Then, quite possibly,

You will <u>Know Yourself</u>, <u>Love Yourself</u> & <u>Appreciate Yourself</u> perhaps, for the first time.

Roy

THE DISTRACTED YOGI
PARTS I—IV
HOW I RECLAIMED MY BLISS
AFTER BRAIN INJURY & TRAUMA

BY M G DESGAGNE

Thank-you for your support! You will get better.....

Michele

A Note about this Book:

Some * names, and certain details have been changed or altered to protect the privacy and integrity of those persons.

The opinions expressed herein are those solely of the author.

This book is not intended to be a substitute for medical treatment or advice. Please seek the guidance of a qualified medical practitioner where appropriate.

ISBN: 1484953258
ISBN-13: 978-1484953259

DEDICATION

With Love and respect: To my Mom.
Even though we don't talk anymore because we really don't
get along very well, you're still the Warrior Queen to me. You
raised three Warrior Princesses and three Warrior Princes. I am
forever grateful to you for all your sacrifices for us - Your
Warrior Tribe.

CONTENTS

FAQ'S (FREQUENTLY ASKED QUESTIONS)

Q. Why write this book?

A. To answer the following questions common to anyone who has an Acquired Brain-Injury, but also too for their loved-ones & curious others.

Q. What is at the core of our (those with BI) anxiety towards the *outside world*?

A. Not feeling understood & that we are alone.

Q. What obstacles, in this *outer world*, are our most difficult to overcome?

A. i) Lack of understanding i.e. getting blamed for our condition &

ii) Lack of empathy from others.

Q. What do we fear the most about our *inner world*?

A. That we won't get better & will never really *know* ourselves again.

Q. Why me, why did this happen to me?!

A. Why not YOU?

INTRODUCTION

This book is the end result of monumental effort. Having a Traumatic Brain Injury changes everything; I do not look, act, speak and most obvious to me, don't think like I used to prior to acquiring this condition.

Maybe you have heard Brain Injury described another way? Post-Concussion Syndrome; Concussion; Mild Traumatic Brain Injury; Hit by a bus? Okay that last one is my own personal description but you get my meaning.

Who or what is 'The Distracted Yogi'? It's my description of my 'New Self'. I first thought of myself as *distracted* a short time after being hit by a car while I rode my bike across a quiet side street one Sunday afternoon nearly 11 years ago. You see up until that time I maintained a rigorous living routine of yoga, meditation, sports, hikes, employment, vacations, social functions, relationships, acquaintances & pretty much whatever else I could think of doing.

Friends & family would describe me then as honest, calm, patient, bright, witty, fun, energetic, fit & attractive and, at times, stubborn & opinionated.

This description of my former life is all that remains of it.

Actually, I continue to be stubborn & opinionated, just less so!

I didn't write this book to bring you down or to get a huge helping of pity. It's simply my account of Brain Injury-from the inside, written with what I hope is an appropriate and entertaining balance of candor and humor. What's *not* here is page after page of statistics, medical jargon and/or presumption. Those books have been and continue to be written by qualified (we can hope!) persons.

If you or someone you know has acquired a brain injury; maybe someone you barely associate with or with whom you are deeply attached, then you will get something of value out of this book. I wouldn't have undertaken the task had I not believed completely that others could and would benefit from my story. I know this to be true because I've already heard this from so many others like me and like you. The truth touches everyone.

THANK YOU!

A Brain-Injured person requires a team of people to assist them and in general take care of all of the things that we used to before our *new* life took over.

At times, this *new self* can be unkind, uncaring, and ungrateful and much, much worse; we are really just afraid of what has happened to us!

The people that make up this team, however rag-tag it may be, are real heroes.

They require a strong stomach, short memory span & most importantly, the qualities of kindness, patience & empathy; in short, unconditional love.

So in Gratitude & Love, I Give Huge Thanks to:
Dr. K R Hatlelid & Staff, Family Practice Vancouver, BC,
GF Strong Rehabilitation Ctr., Vancouver, BC,
J Lynne Mann MA, R. Psych (TRG-Creator & Facilitator).
Sol Mongerman - for his book and all of its endless inspiration!

My Dearest Friends & Adopted Family-Tribe; Sheila, Lola, Annette, Anita B., Christina, Kate R., Irene, and Martin & Sammy (a.k.a. The Cats Who Saved My life!).
*Mary, Butch & Carol Nelson, Mike & Charlotte, John & Amy, Vito B., Wayne, Ramona and the many other Shelter Island Marina Boat-People whose names have escaped me!

More Huge Thanks and Appreciation to: Craig Ballantyne; co-editor/contributor of ETR-Early to Rise online newsletter & creator of The Transformation Contest.com

To All My New TC Friends & Friendships- borne out of

the collective struggle to live in accordance with one's own potential; a.k.a. The Rag-Tag Warriors-You People Are Awesome! Thank you, I love you all! XO

A Very Special Thank You to: Stacy McCusker, a.k.a. 'The Faerie-Pixie-Dust-Soul-Sister-Queen' for her intuitive creation-the cover-art for The Distracted Yogi!
You can see Stacy's creations at:
http://www.etsy.com/shop/CosmicArts
& more links and info in the 'Artist's Biography' at the back of this book.
&
My Copy-editor & dear friend Binita Patel, for taking me and *The Distracted Yogi* on, then showing me what a really good read looks like. Contact info:
www.DivineWebWriter.com ,
email Binita@DivineWebWriter.com .
&
Lee, www.IronhorseFormatting.com, for your generous nature & excellent work-ethic. Thank you!
& In Gratitude;
Cover-Lotus-Blossom, used with permission, by:
www.SweetClipArt.com .

PART I

BRAIN INJURY VS BLISS

CHAPTER I-WHAT'S HAPPENING TO ME?!

April –June 2002

"Loss of memory is often associated with brain injury and can greatly contribute to the feelings of confusion and disassociation that you may feel upon discovering yourself in a changed condition. Though it can also serve to insulate you from knowledge of the seriousness of your condition, it can be, in itself, a great cause for dread and dismay". From: Objects in the mirror are closer than they appear, by Sol Mongerman.

Life would not be nearly as interesting as it is if it were not for irony.

How ironic it was then that I should be hit by a car while riding my bike on a Sunday. Not a Monday or a Friday or any other work day but rather on my day off. I had commuted to work primarily by bike for nearly 10 years without really even a sniff of an accident until that day. It was in Vancouver, BC April 8, 2002.

I would not return to work.

It has taken my mind this long to formulate my thoughts into a readily accessed stream of consciousness but actually to be completely accurate, I did write about 200 pages in journal form over the course of 3 or 4 years but lost all that data some time ago. I didn't take that loss very well but then I don't handle disappointments as well as I used to.

This is not the life I would have chosen for myself initially but, now that I'm *here,* and no longer *where I was,* I can live with it. In fact, I can now say that in many ways I'm new and improved.

Life wasn't always this way...the way it is *now.*   In

examining My Goals Comparison Chart below one can quickly understand who I *was*. It has taken many years, and much drama has transpired for me to be able to state with absolute inner-belief and confidence that "I'm okay."

Goals Comparison Chart

March 2002	April 2002
1.Climb Denali before age 45.	Walk for at least 5 mins.
2.Make the Dragonboat Team	Stop falling over
3.Bike & Boat tour of Denmark	Face my bike again
4.Upgrade my education	Learn to tell time
5.Upgrade my job	Speak in complete sentences
6.Visit friends in Norway	Leave the house

I had been a daily meditator and practiced Mindfulness living for 7 years prior to the accident but that all changed in a moment.

Below is a good example of my physical, mental and emotional states before and immediately after the accident:

Internal & External Experience

BEFORE	-Accident-	AFTER
• Self-Aware		Unaware Disconnected
• Centered & Whole		Scattered & Broken
• Self-Confident		Fragile & Fractured
• Social & Outgoing		Isolated & Passive
• Focused		Distracted
• Fit & Active		Atrophied & Sedentary
• Sense of Humor		Blank & Morose
Self-Sufficient		Dependant
• Vibrant & Energetic		Dull & Exhausted
• Articulate		Incoherent

The next several chapters begin to create a larger, more detailed mental picture for you, of what my inner experience was like immediately after the accident. Some of my descriptions may not mean anything to you at first but I encourage you to hang in there with me as I struggle, even now, to understand what was happening to me then, within my damaged self as these early realities eventually merge into what is the *bigger picture*.

After the initial shock and realization that I was a changed person, my story really picks up and so too the telling of it will become more familiar to you in terms of structure and layout.

I'll take you through this journey with me, as a companion of sorts, to bear witness to the confusion and heartbreak and the ultimate freedom-that is brain injury.

April –June 2002
Being In A FOG

I didn't realize that I was in a dense fog-like state of awareness for the first six weeks. Sure, my head felt thick, and

I knew that I wasn't explaining myself as clearly and that I just couldn't seem to find the words anymore, but I also knew that they were in there somewhere. I'd seen my doctor many times over the course of the initial six weeks, and towards the end I had confessed to him that I'd only just realized that I had been eating cookies, and nothing else, that I was aware of.

Can't Tell Time Anymore

I was always missing appointments which made no sense because I had been using a day timer for 7 + years and knew how to keep to an appointment or commitment. It wasn't that I was just late or getting lost, yes those things were happening too, but it was that I just didn't remember that I had the appointment to begin with.

I didn't seem to be able to remember to even look at my Day-Timer or check my PDA. I'm sure that I'd received reminder calls, but that didn't seem to matter either as I'd still miss the appointment. I'd be very distressed about it, and to add to the confusion was my suspicion that I could no longer understand the clock or its purpose. What did it mean? The hands and the face with the numbers, what did it all mean?! Studying them intently and then waiting for the clarity to kick in didn't seem to help one bit; I just couldn't seem to grasp its meaning, and I'd eventually understand too, that I could no longer feel *the passage of time*-it seemed to stand still in its place unmoved by the external events of life. Not even the natural phenomenon of sunrises and sunsets changed my inner world sensation of *time not moving*. This remains that way to this day.

I Have Cats?!

Initially, I didn't remember having cats. Mary, my partner at the time, would visit daily, and one day she simply announced that I needed to scoop out the litter box. It took some time for me to figure out what this meant. What was she referring to? Only after she proceeded to clean it out, did I then understand but only in a very vague and disconnected way. What was going on?! I know that I'm not a stupid or lazy person, yet Mary was always getting mad at me, or so it seemed.

Much, much later it would occur to me that one of my cats had been extremely ill. He had been vomiting for weeks, maybe months and I had not cleaned up any of it. It had dried into unrecognizable clumps throughout my house and, at that time I was renting a 350 sq. ft. Houseboat. It would have been impossible not to see all the piles of vomit, yet I was completely unaware of anything being amiss. One day, Mary just showed up with a carpet steam-cleaner and took care of the huge mess.

How could I not even have smelled it? I'd had a keen sense of smell and I'd realized too that I hadn't recalled seeing anything or hearing anything either. Unfortunately these realizations didn't last and my awareness of things would quickly lapse back into the fog. This pattern of having a moment or two of clarity, then memory regression would come to dominate my mental and emotional states for the next several years.

Prior to the accident, Mary and I saw one another infrequently; she worked full-time and I was always busy with work, sports and other social commitments. However, now she was over much more often, taking care of me, my home and my cats.

The First Of Many Doctors' Appointments
Those first few appointments were, from what I can remember of them, mostly about reporting the pain and discomfort and the unusual goings on in my life in general. The pain on the left side of my head had really started to bother me, as did my left shoulder and both of my lower legs and feet. I could not comprehend why my feet continued to hurt so badly especially since the accident was weeks ago by then. My other observations regarding time and space

confusion were difficult to report because my ability to communicate anything effectively had been severely stunted. I no longer possessed the proper perspectives of time and space.

As the appointments progressed, so too did my doctor's concern for my condition and prospects of complete recovery.

My family doctor is a beautiful, patient and caring person and without his tenacity, I can't imagine what may have happened to me in an over-burdened medical system. I could only extrapolate through the many frequent horror stories I'd often hear from others, as my own recovery journey progressed.

Living On The Water

At the time of my accident I was living in a marina. I'd thought of it as a huge blessing, because I loved all the varied forms of wildlife. More importantly, being close to the water was the biggest bonus to the lifestyle. I'd had a very hectic life, and at times an extremely stressful job, so this place became my refuge long before the accident.

When I'd first moved onto the houseboat, sometime prior to the accident, it took me a few weeks to 'get my sea legs'. After the initial breaking in period, eventually the ground did stop moving beneath me, especially when I was on the 'hard'; as boat-people like say in reference to 'land.'

One of the best things about living on the water, as opposed to 'on the hard', was the family atmosphere; my neighbors *were* my family. We talked every day and there were endless shared meals and massive communal gatherings on weekends. It was the level of community that I'd become so drawn into, something that was absent from the condo experience in the city, one that I had opted-out of a few years earlier.

I'd felt like I was coming home to my 'cabin at the lake' whenever I'd return from work. As soon as I'd reach the road to the marina the city noises would abate and the sounds of the ocean would overlay to the point of dominance. Suddenly, it was just gulls, bald eagles and crows; then the clanking of masts and the ever so faint smells of diesel fuel and paint from the boatyard that was attached to the marina. Across form the marina office was the 'boatyard of broken dreams' where there were several acres of stored, broken and abandoned vessels of various types and sizes. This was sad to me but interesting too; who are these people, and what were their dreams?

My houseboat was situated at C Dock, the furthest dock from the office. I'd really loved the feeling of being free while striding down the ramp, hearing the sounds of my feet on the hardwood planks. It really was such a special place to live; work-life was quickly forgotten and my sensory-existence became wrapped up in the immediate serenity of this place, it was the perfect environment for me then.

Other Strange Stuff & Behaviours

All of the awe-inspiring beauty of my home environment was lost to me immediately after the accident.

My neighbors would often remind me whenever we spoke, that we had just had the present conversation the day before and that they had noticed I was sleeping a lot, all day in fact. They had plenty of questions for me, but I could offer few if any answers. Sleeping all day?! I'd thought that they must be mistaken; I was certain that I'd had a life and was busy living it, even though I had absolutely no recollection of participating in it.

It was around that time, six weeks to 2 months post injury that I'd noticed how difficult it was for me to remain awake. Also, if I stood up I'd quickly fall over usually to my right which made tying my shoe laces impossible so my slippers became my main footwear of choice out of necessity (although I don't believe it was a conscious choice). It may be possible that I'd somehow been re-experiencing more of that 'sea legs' phenomenon, except that the ground moved under me no matter where I was or what I was doing. At first the vertigo lasted days, then weeks, then months until I'd eventually just accepted that I'd need to simply co-exist with it.

The act of walking felt odd. I was sure that I was walking in a straight line but felt as though my body was pointed off to my right-side and I would continually need to verify this by checking the direction my feet were pointed towards! I was continually stopping and correcting what felt like was a 'being off course' problem.

My internal compass was somehow skewed and this problem lead to the more disconcerting issue of getting disoriented and lost in places that I'd previously been familiar with.

Going to the airport to pick up a friend was a huge source of stress because not only were the crowds difficult to navigate through, but I couldn't remember where to go nor did I comprehend the signage. Asking for help or directions was useless because I wasn't able to focus on the answers long enough to grasp their meaning. I also felt too afraid of people to approach anyone and besides, I'd thought, what would I say? Life was now the *sensation* that people, and everything else in general, moved around above me in circles. There was no beginning or end, just massive confusion.

Adding to these difficulties was the ever present physical sensation of nausea; it was constant, at nearly every waking moment.

My pre-accident life had been rife with allergies and asthma symptoms; perhaps I'd thought then that I was experiencing something like that of typical allergy symptoms? My brain could not hold on any thought for long, so the awareness of symptomology would quickly fade from my mind. This made it impossible to paint a complete picture of health about myself to me, or others.

Mush Mind

Many symptoms came and went from my awareness during those first few years. There were times when someone would point out behaviour or a reaction in me which would hold my interest for a millisecond, but then would melt back into the void of mush and grayness.

Grayness and mush, this *was* my mind and it no longer seemed connected to me. It was something outside of my awareness now, something *over there* somewhere but not, *in here*. My experience of *thinking* was a *sensation of vagueness* and I believe that this state of being vague contributes greatly to our *appearance of vagueness,* and may even account for why many brain injured persons look like they are depressed, but are perhaps actually more *stunned* especially in the early stages post-injury.

I'm Not Right

I was completely cognizant of these changes in me, and I would continually remind people of this by saying "this is not like me", or "I'm usually very good at this stuff" and "I just can't remember right now" and the often repeated "I know that I know this"!

I remember the feelings of frustration too; maybe this was grief at its earliest beginnings? I knew something was off with me and my thinking, I'd constantly be saying to my friends and family, "I'm not right, I'm just not right!"

It was a very strange existence for me then and as I'd drift in and out of awareness I'd remember nothing specific about people or places except the persistent impressions of distraction and perplexity. I would use that last word often when attempting to explain my state to myself and others especially doctors and specialists that: "I feel as though I'm in a permanent state of perplexity." I never felt then that I was completely understood by anyone during this time and I'd believed that no one could really, honestly or scientifically, *get* what had happened to me or how it had affected my internal state of being.

These feelings of frustration would later morph into still greater frustration, eventually anger, then grief but those emotions would need much, much more time to develop completely within my psyche.

Where Are Those Sounds Coming From?

Another bizarre phenomenon which to me seemed to be occurring off somewhere in the distant background were strange sounds and voices. I could never seem to pinpoint their origin either. These *sounds* would start out as vague, low imperceptible signals like a radio not quite tuned in to its proper channel, then slowly but gradually they would become more specific like that of someone talking or laughing. I would look around the room or, if I were outside, would physically twist around trying to locate the source of the noises often looking skyward, as if expecting to see a plane or something that I could pin the noises onto. It seemed to me that there were conversations and disturbances constantly going on in a continuous circular-like pattern somewhere above my head.

Undoubtedly my behaviour would have perplexed whomever I was speaking with but in truth, if I was with someone I already knew, by that time, they would have come to expect this kind of odd behaviour from me.

It was much, much later in my recovery when I'd realized that those 'noises and disturbances' where actually coming directly from the person that I'd been speaking with all along.

I No Longer Feel Safe In The World

Conversing with strangers and others became a huge source of anxiety for me, so consequently I'd rarely speak to anyone except those people whom I already *recognized*.

Going out on my own became a terrifying experience. I'd begun to experience that people in general seemed scary, especially since I'd barely recognized some of my friends, and still at other times *no one* looked familiar to me.

I *knew* that I was somehow altered and this knowledge became a huge source of anxiety within me. I no longer felt safe. Self-confidence and self-belief were now strangely absent from my demeanor, stemming directly from my inability to adequately understand or express myself. My thoughts seemed stuck in their place so nothing in my awareness moved or flowed anymore - not physically, mentally, emotionally or spiritually, so I not only felt inert but looked that way too.

As a result of this mental block, conversations with outsiders usually went very badly. I would feel afraid just to be out in public so when speaking became necessary, say perhaps to the stock-person in the grocery store, I would simply freeze-up. The words that I knew I needed to speak would not come out of my mouth, and if I'd actually managed to say something intelligent the next logical sentence wouldn't form in my mind; the information stream that used to be automatic had run dry.

I'd frantically search for the word or words or frame of reference, but could not connect with the vital information that I knew was *in there,* somewhere.

Another example would be like if you were trying to cross a stream but the roads are all washed out. You know if you just get to the other side you'll be fine but finding a 'bridge' to crossover to it, is the key. The longer you search for this connection, this cross-over to safety, the more anxious you become because the answers are not coming, and the connection is not being made, so in the end you are just frozen in place. You cannot move until you get the signal that you've been waiting for, some information, a word, anything for the way out, but it never comes and you feel so afraid because you may never get to that safe place; the place of knowing, where all the answers are just waiting for you to come in and get them.

My new self-reality was really a convergence of issues, each issue having real-life compounding and devastating side-effects.

I'll Be Fine!

I had to get myself to appointments soon after the accident so I'd continued to drive myself to these engagements. I cringe at the thought of that now and believe that I was extremely fortunate to have not gotten into any subsequent accidents.

I'd acted as if I was going to be fine in a few weeks and that these things would all settle down eventually and very soon. I'd get back on track; back to my life, the life I loved and enjoyed and back to myself again, the person I loved and admired and respected.

I acted as normal as *I remembered myself to be*, as quickly as possible so driving to and from appointments became one way of getting back to all things normal.

This period of self-reliance didn't last long however; I would soon be relieved of my driving privileges which in actuality gave me a huge sense of relief.

I'd carried on as though nothing had changed such as attempting to cook meals for myself but those attempts always ending badly. It didn't matter that I had been sleeping almost 23 hours a day or that I didn't remember having cats and that I was unaware of time passing or, more precisely, the concept of time; trying to look and act as if all things *were* normal anchored me to the idea that I was OK.

The first time I'd noticed something awry with my cooking skills, which used to be proficient, was when attempting to make a protein shake. Drinking a protein shake every morning had been a well- established routine in my life for many, many years.

I'd been very particular about what foods I put in my body and was primarily eating a vegetable based diet along with organic meats, usually chicken and fish. I preferred certified organic foods and made the weekly trip to the local farmer's market for the freshest food I could find.

Eating well and being well was like a religion to me, and nothing was more important to me than my daily rituals of meditation, reading great books, practicing mindfulness and authenticity of character, being active in the outdoors, travel & adventure, consuming only fresh and sustainable food, showing up for my friends & family and being great at my job; a job, which afforded me the luxury to participate in the many activities that gave me so much joy.

By the time of the accident I'd already made huge changes in my attitude and life so that I could enjoy it to the fullest.

At the time of my injury:
- I'd been a non-drinker for 11 years and a non-smoker for 10.
- I was an avid hiker and backpacking was also another favorite pastime. I'd been working out at a gym regularly for nearly 20 years by then as well.
- I'd tried a vegetarian diet for 3 or 4 years and had only just recently added meat protein back into my diet and would later do several more flip-flops.
- I'd become engrossed in the practice of meditation and mindfulness as a way of living 7 years prior to the brain injury.
- I'd sought out many different paths, ideas and models of living; I was a seeker of knowledge and my life revolved around this central theme.

Okay! Back to the protein shake...

I couldn't figure out how to operate the blender or what to fill it with but I knew on some level that this was a daily habit but that was about all I had retained of it, and without more information, like the whys or how's, I'd simply abandon the former ritual.

That exact moment, *distracted* and unremarkable, became a tangible place in time that I would later reflect back on and identify as when the first of many of my former health-focused behaviours were abandoned. I could say too that the instant my head struck the windshield of the car, well, perhaps that was the moment everything changed, which it did. However, what I'm trying to pinpoint for you is the precise 30 seconds where my former life faded into the realm of memory only.

This precise moment, but a flash in time, gave birth to my new coping behaviours. Some were without their tangible connections to my former healthy lifestyle. These were the ugly, dysfunctional relics from my distant past that would eventually return to become my primary coping strategies.

Why Doesn't This Make Any Sense To Me?

Conversations with others became increasingly impossible. The problem of not being able to pinpoint the source of all the exterior noise and interference, created other challenges like not being able to follow a conversation. I would try so hard to just concentrate on the person's face or eyes or mouth but could not focus long enough to grasp the meaning or purpose of the conversation.

If there were more than one person talking my brain quickly became overloaded with sensory input thus experiencing the phenomenon of *thought flooding*. My brain felt utterly ready to explode which would feel both terrifying and painful, often causing me to retreat from people without any explanation, fleeing in full on flight mode.

It was a very confusing time…for me and for those closest to me.

I wasn't able to communicate anymore. It was difficult to find my voice to talk then find the words or concepts I was trying to express. Conversations would start but not finish. My voice would simply trail off somewhere as my mind searched for the word or words only to become lost, off track and confused about why I was standing where I was, talking I'd guess, to the person in front of me. Sometimes I'd say out of frustration "Why can't I speak properly?! I know how to have an intelligent conversation with someone! This is so frustrating!"

Outwardly I'd look lost, stunned or just blank. Often people asked if I was depressed but I really didn't know what I was feeling. I didn't really feel anything for more than a few seconds and in general, couldn't hang on to feelings long enough to form a complete thought, much less express it before it too would simply dissolve.

Nothing made sense anymore.

Thoughts would get stuck in their place with nothing else to attach to. It was so painful at the time but then quickly forgotten like every other thought, quickly just fading to gray. This problem, of poor communication and inhibited comprehension persisted, lasting for years having an enormous destabilizing effect on me, and becoming the driving force behind my fragile and plummeting self-confidence.

The losses just kept coming although I hadn't recognised them as losses…yet.

Disconnect From Self

The early days and months after the injury for me were fraught with anxiety, and I would conclude that this was one feeling that sometimes became a constant where no others could take hold. Mercifully though, *no feeling* would last for very long in my awareness before the familiar sensation of graying-out would take over.

This lack of 'being', coupled with the loss of feeling connected to my inner-self was difficult to describe, or comprehend during this time. My pre-accident sense of self, revolved around feeling centered and connected which was the foundation of *me*; where I started and ended. This was the vibrating essence of my connection to everything else too.

I believe this inner experience of self is unique in feeling to every person; It's the inside story of me, and of you, of who we believe ourselves to be.

But now it too was gone. I was without anything solid to grasp onto- to call *me*. I'd hung onto the belief that 'I' would return at any time and was certain that 'I' was coming back if I could just be patient, "the Michelle that is OK will show up and things would get back to normal and my life would continue on its natural, predicable trajectory." Each and every day, for years, whenever I woke up, I'd expect the real *me* to have returned, and when the inevitable reality hit me, that I hadn't come back, deep despair would then soon follow, never lasting long at first, but eventually, much later, grief would take hold.

Denial of loss, I'd later understand, played an important role in keeping the hope alive within me and that, that hope would ultimately carry me through some future difficulties. But my injured brain could not hang on to anything longer than a moment or two either, so denial pairs with injury to preserves one's motivation and drive to keep going. This is one of the ingenious and automatic means by which our brain protects and preserves itself during these episodes of recovery from trauma.

Becoming More Aware Of My Body And Of Pain

Time passed and my brain continued it's very slow but determined healing process.

By months 2-3, mid June 2002, I had become aware of the terrible pain in my left shoulder. It had made hard contact with the hood of the car that had struck me. Along with the rest of my body, I'd travelled up the hood of the car with my head and back towards the cars' windshield, then, slamming up against it hard-then eventually being catapulted back in the direction I'd come from- landing in heap on the ground a short distance in front of the car.

I hadn't realized that I wasn't really using that arm and that it was just hanging at my side most of the time. I was engaged in a few therapies by now like Massage and Chiropractic including Cranial Sacral therapy and it was these therapists who I'd remembered pointing this out to me. Much later, when re-reading some of the mountains of medical information generated by a subsequent insurance claim, my family doctor had also made the suspected diagnosis of a separated shoulder injury (among other injuries) long before I felt any pain or at least had the awareness of pain.

Immediately after being struck by the car and within moments of returning to consciousness I'd felt the excruciating pain in my feet and lower legs. I didn't remember feeling the rest of my body with the exception of those places and possibly the places on my head where it had contacted the car's hood and windshield. Anyone who has experienced this would agree, those very first moments of awareness can be so confusing and disorienting; my first thoughts were "it's very dark in here", then, "Where am I"?

Slowly, very, very slowly did I regain the awareness of feeling myself in my body and as more time passed more physical symptoms would manifest as pain.

One such symptom was that my head felt like a throbbing mass which constantly ached and was extremely itchy. I became so intolerant of the constant, unrelenting pain that I confessed to my family doctor that I was going to shave all the hair off my head out of desperation for some relief. Gratefully, he talked me out it and instead prescribed a pain remedy which eventually made the situation more tolerable.

A somewhat milder level of head pain persists to this day, nearly 11 years post-accident yet I consider myself to be very lucky. My injuries could have been so much worse. At the time however, I'd often lament that dying wasn't the worst case scenario because *surviving* was so difficult.

I'd believed that years of dedication to meditating and yoga, cleaning up my life and 'living harmoniously with the earth' would somehow protect me and give me a head start in recovery. I'd get better and return to my former life and carry on as though this were just some minor inconvenience to be overcome and 'worked through'. I had been through other similar challenges in the past including car accidents, sports injuries and a few lingering health issues. I considered myself a fighter so not only would I get better but also faster than most others in the same predicament.

That was my prevailing attitude at the time, which lasted about 4 weeks, not too shabby in retrospect.

I'd recognized too, that while I appeared to have developed the tremendous capacity to cope with adversity, I had no point of reference with which to deal with this new damaged-self reality. I couldn't connect the experience of being brain-injured to anything from my past; no prior experience of difficulty or challenge could match up to my present reality. It was like nothing I'd ever been through, and I'd thought then, that I'd already been through a lot in my life.

Vision Anomalies

Visual problems are a frequent and common side-effect of brain injury.

As a small child, being called 'Eagle-Eyes' was probably one of the first nicknames I can recall. There were several others but not quite so complimentary!

I loved knowing that I was good at spotting things when other kids, especially my siblings, didn't. From my young perspective, starting life as the middle child in a family with five other siblings required special skillsets to set me apart and to ensure I survived the experience!

There is unseen damage with a brain injured person that is not always obvious to the casual observer, or to persons within their inner circle of friends and family.

Within me is a lifetime of mostly small experiences and impressions which have built up a foundation of self-knowledge, and this in turn has resulted in generating self-confidence and self-belief. It's a unique *inside* perspective of one's self which is something that we all possess but rarely exhibit to the outside world; the sum total of these beliefs and impressions making up the internal *idea* of who we believe we are. These self-concepts, which I'd cling to for years afterwards, were no longer accurate; they'd eventually come to represent me as *the time before the injury*.

This injury event would become the new demarcation point of my life, representing the before and after story of Michelle. And the *after*, it soon seemed, was a bottomless crevice of misery. It was one that I, along with more than a few loved-ones who were closest to me, had gradually gotten sucked into; this was the void that is the world of brain injury.

Okay, Back To The Vision Problems!

After the injury, 'Eagle-Eyes' Michelle no longer existed. The clarity of my visual world changed in an instant as everything in my field of vision became blurred. My view of the world was akin to looking through a dirty window covered with dirty streaks all fuzzy and grey. I would consciously try to refocus my eyes, thinking that if I concentrated then blinked enough times, things would return to their former clarity. It never worked however, and consequently my outer world took on the impression that a permanently oppressive-like bank of fog had descended upon it.

And whenever the outside world was darker, like dusk, dawn and night-time, then it was nearly impossible for me to see and discern objects like whether they were near or far-off in the distance.

Double-Vision

Double-vision manifested primarily when I would try to read something such as my day timer, a book, a newspaper or a doctor's note etc. Reading, once a daily habit of joy and relaxation, was quickly abandoned as words appeared shadowed and wouldn't stay in one place, but rather jumped around the page forming new, unpronounceable ones. Even if I could have read, there was the problem with comprehension, or lack of thereof.

Nothing made sense. I could no longer figure out the meaning or purpose of things like a clock or my watch, and I'd soon stop wearing around my wrist because it was pointless to do so.

My home was filled with books. I'd read spiritual scripture, inspirational, quantum theory, mathematics, travel, business & entrepreneur models, practical how to and Do-It –Yourself manuals, tales of explorers like Ernest Shackleton, Cpt. James Cook and many others, but my absolute favorites were of the cookbook variety. I read those books cover to cover then started over again; they captivated my attention like nothing else on the bookshelf.

Not only was my comprehension and vision affected, but each time I would try to hold a book to read it, I'd experience severe nausea. It would also happen if I leaned over the table to read my day timer or any document, thus the act of reading declined along with the immense enjoyment it had once produced.

I Can't Handle All The Noise!

I never watched much TV back then, but now it suddenly became just irritating noise. I usually only watched the morning news bites and the weather channel, but now these too just felt irritating, like microphone feedback or the bizarre sounds one hears when their cell phone is going out of range, similar to radio static.

Listening to music was unbearable. It just sounded to me, like someone trying to talk over a lot of noise, or that they, the vocalists were trying to out yell one another. The music would fade in and out not connected to the words, which was absolutely excruciating to me.

Often I couldn't figure out the location of the noise. Like when people were speaking to me, I didn't connect the sounds to their source. The sounds were just 'out there' without purpose or meaning. It was all just interference to me. I was overwhelmed with all this *outer* stimulation which I could not seem to escape.

To this day I cannot tolerate much in the way of loud noises. Perhaps they only appear to be loud to me but whatever their true level, I continue to be sensitive to the everyday sounds of others just living out their lives.

What's That Smell?!

I could just say that all my senses were dulled, but that wouldn't quite cover it. The experience of losing the connection to, and sense of enjoyment derived from, my sight, hearing and other senses affected me profoundly.

I'm referring to my life mainly at 2 to 6 months post injury, but in some cases, years passed before these senses would return to quasi-normal, and while some symptoms did disappear over time, others morphed into more complex problems.

I wasn't really aware of any changes to my sense of smell, until I began to smell something awful all of the time. This smell was a lot like the stench of rotting garbage, and I felt like I was living inside a dumpster. It, this putrid smell, permeated my immediate environment to the point where my clothes and body would reek of it. I'd be constantly asking the people around me if they too could smell it, but the answer was always the same, "Garbage? Ah, no I don't think so." They would then list all the things that they *could* smell but garbage was never one of them.

I think it's possible that this unrelenting foul odor may have contributed to my lack of interest in eating. I mentioned earlier that gourmet cookies were my main source of nutrition for those first 4-6 weeks, and maybe I did eat other foods but for the memory gaps, I may never know.

During those first few weeks my neighbors would often leave food outside my door. This beautiful tradition started before the accident when I was working long hours, and would get home late, and then be up again before dawn to start yet another long work day. When the weather was really cold, I would arrive home to a freshly built fire in the woodstove, the main heat source on my houseboat. My cats would be so content that they hardly noticed my comings and goings, provided the fire was crackling. Fun times!

Post-accident however, everything was much, much different and while the food tradition continued, I was no longer aware it.

Why Don't I Drink Alcohol?!
Occasionally I would literally stumble outside just to get

some air and try to remember why I'd chosen to live in such a place. I would sit outside on the tiny deck attached to the houseboat and stare off at nothing, until the sounds of sea birds broke the spell.

Even though I had been clean & sober for nearly 11 years at the time of the accident, I remembered nothing of this previous life.

Boat life to me seemed to attract a certain kind of person; hard drinking males, but not restricted to just men, party animals and other seemingly lost-soul types; there were couples and single women too, and but for a few exceptions, they tended to be softer, gentler and quieter types.

I'd not remembered being a sober person. I felt perplexed most of the time and would often ask myself, "Why would I choose to live in a place like this?" I hadn't been able to figure out the logic behind my decision to live in a community overpopulated with drunks, when I appeared not to drink! It didn't make any sense and I'd concluded that I must have been in a very bad way emotionally, prior to making the move to my current home.

Eventually I did remember a few more details about my former life with the assistance of my clean and sober friends, their memories back-filling some of the gaping holes of my own.

When I reflect back on this strange time, I'm struck by how fortunate I was to be living where I was. These boat-life people became my new family; they took care of me when my birth family couldn't. They provided 24 hour coverage and care because that's the kind of community-oriented people they were; everyone just pitched in without being asked to.

My partner at the time, Mary, was traumatized as well when she had witnessed the accident, and said that she was certain that I was dead at the scene. She never talked about it much because it was probably too painful for her to continually relive, what by then, had become in her mind just awful, galvanized moments of horror.

We had only dated for a few months prior to the accident, and had not yet established the relationship as having long term potential. Yet after the accident she stayed and took care of me, my pets, my needs and everything else too. She worked full-time, but I don't really remember much about that now, but I do recall her bringing home take-out Chinese, steam cleaning the vomit covered carpets and starting the fire day after day. She did occasionally complain about things, but saw her mounting dissatisfactions going nowhere, as they would continually come up against my blank and trance-like state of being.

I'm forever in debt to her for staying because I know it wasn't easy for her.

Whatever we had, whatever potential existed for us before, was no more because the 'I' in I was no more. The new relationship reality was very bleak; one day post-accident and I didn't act, look, speak or think like I had the day before.

In less than a single moment of time I'd become a stranger to myself, and to all those who knew me.

CHAPTER II-A New Identity

Mid June 2002-February 2003

"Now you know how I feel"...from well-meaning friends & family.

The first time someone suggested to me that I was now privy to their formerly misunderstood existence, I'd thought honestly...nothing, but I felt very hurt and misunderstood too. Much later though I *was* able to find a reply, but I'd also recognize that these people who were close to me had already experienced a lifetime of challenge.

Now, I needed them to understand my challenges too. To me, their lives were like an ongoing experiment of carefully constructed coping skills specific to their challenges, whereas I'd had only one moment to adjust, they had been adjusting and perfecting their coping strategies for decades.

But the emotions of hurt and betrayal took time to formulate into words which were percolating, all the while, deep inside my psyche. At first, they appeared as just vague feelings of hurt and angst, then suddenly like a geyser and all at once, I'd erupt in an explosion of grief, then it was done for now, all but forgotten except for the residue which was always anxiety.

This idea of me being misunderstood and persecuted would become another recurrent theme in my ever-developing, fragile mental and emotional self.

Why Would I Need To Go *There*?!

June 2002 brought many new stressors. First, my Doctor referred me to a place called GF Strong Rehabilitation Center, a place I was familiar with. In a previous relationship, I had driven my partner to and from her work there, the very same GF Strong Rehab Center, and I'd often remarked then, how sad I felt for the patients. The typical in-patient there was severely immobilized either with brain injury or spinal cord injury. Looking back, before my injury, I'd counted myself in with the fortunate and unbroken souls.

So, it was with this perspective of the place, which had remained in my mind, and was there still when the Intake Nurse called for the pre-appointment interview. I was stunned. Why would I need to go there?! I was deeply offended and disappointed with my family doctor. I just could not understand the reasoning; there could be no rational explanation so it had to be a mistake of gigantic proportions. What was he, my doctor, thinking?!

I remember stumbling over words, and not being able to express myself. The nurse was never going to get what I was trying to spit out. In my mind, this was a huge mistake, and I shouldn't be here. However, the interview commenced without missing a beat.

As the phone call progressed, and after what may have been some time, I only recalled one question, "how are you doing with money?" I think I may have stopped breathing after that. How could she possibly know that I hadn't been able to track money or account for my spending? And that every time I looked in my wallet, usually to pay for something, it was empty. There was nothing in there but a black hole? Why and how did she even think to ask about money?!

Immediately after hanging up from the call, I'd felt devastated. I knew I was angry, but it all spilled out as grief. I had immediately picked up the phone to call my friend Sheila. She worked in health care so maybe she could help me, and in turn, help my doctor sort this thing out.

She understood completely, and by the end of that conversation so did I, or so I thought I did. Sheila explained that although I had been expecting a call from a neurologist, (my presumption), my doctor was helping me by referring me to a *team* of specialists. She had been sneaky about the facts, but it worked, and I'd felt better because I was finally going to get some real help. The reality was that I was completely clueless about what was coming at this point.

You Have A Brain Injury!

Very soon after that I entered through the front doors of GF Strong, I was feeling very afraid and very uncertain.

Everything there, the wide hallways, the plentiful staff, the bold signage and even the lady staffing the reception booth seemed foreign and intimidating. Since the accident, I hadn't spent much time out of my home except for several weekly appointments to places I had been to in my *former* life. This place was completely unknown, and to me represented sadness and tragedy; what was someone like me going to possibly get out of this place?

I managed to get myself to the reception person, but like many encounters with new people, I was unable to speak through the muddiness of my thoughts. Luckily for me, she automatically knew this, and thus her efficiency overshadowed my babbling. What was my name? Thankfully, that was the only question; I'd been checked-in and admitted without my even knowing it!

Social occasions where I might be required to speak were especially stressful then. If the only thing required was a simple hello, okay I might be able manage, but beyond that the situation was absolutely terrifying.

The damage to my brain had stunted my ability to anticipate what happens next in any and all situations. In conversations, these skills or nuances are sometimes referred to as social cues and mine were gone. No more cues or the capability to carry on the most basic of conversations. I didn't know that they were gone and I would just experience their absence as anxiety. This deficiency of communication, created the temporary belief in me that the outside world unfriendly, so best to be avoided altogether.

Once seated in the waiting room of GF Strong, I felt that I could relax a bit. Like all new situations and their purpose, the reasons for being there would simply evaporate from my awareness. I would wait unaware of the 'What, Where, How or Why' but rather I'd feel as though life were like a series of suspended moments in time.

It's funny to me that I remember so little of that first day and the subsequent follow-ups, yet, the first few minutes of that first day seem so vivid in my memory.

I do recall the initial intake process I think, because I was required to get my photo taken. I'd later think about how terrified I must have looked, if my face was even able to reflect back my inner anguish with any accuracy.

I was introduced to many people but only remember the primary Care Team person assigned to me, Radha. She was gentle and kind and I felt very safe in her company.

The rest of that first day was a blur with the exception of one conversation. At the end of my first day Radha, sat me down and stated simply "you have a brain injury". I was sure that she was yelling and I didn't get what she was saying, so I asked her to repeat it. So she did and I was completely caught off guard, a brain injury?! At the time, that seemed impossible, ridiculous and utterly out there in left field.

No More Driving For You!

Slowly, very slowly, this new reality began to sink into me. My driving privileges were quickly suspended per Radha's recommendations & based on the results from something called a 'visual field' test which meant from herein I was to ride the ministry of health sponsored- 'Handi-Dart' to and from all appointments. I'm fairly certain that most communities have some version of the 'Handi-Dart', and, even more confident that most people never expect that they would ever need to book a ride on one. I know I didn't but there I was riding the Handi-dart and feeling more than just ok about it, I was actually relieved not to have to drive anymore.

There had been some close calls behind the wheel as I was slow to react to traffic stopped ahead of me. I had known *something* was wrong but hadn't yet concluded the obvious. My attention seemed to wander, and my vision issues further complicated my driving abilities. I couldn't seem to locate the source of the many frequent sirens until the moment the emergency vehicle was upon me, plus I'd felt incapable of making good decisions or more accurately *any* decision. I no longer knew what to do or how to drive and continually became lost and disoriented in traffic. Maps were useless, and so ceased to have any meaning.

I felt something very primal inside, security or maybe safety, whenever I rode the Handi-dart, whatever the feeling was exactly, it allowed me to finally relax.

The Challenges Of Public Transportation

Riding the public transit system is not a hardship in my mind, now or prior to my accident. Once I'd moved onto the houseboat I'd made the decision to use the transit system over riding my bike, as the bike route was fraught with dangers. It would have been necessary to cross several tricky bridges, which at rush hour were choked with antsy, impatient commuters so best avoided altogether.

So taking the bus and the Skytrain, Vancouver's version of the EL, was a preferable way to starting my day, rather than battling it out with the car people. Besides that, they had an unfair advantage over the bike people and we, the bike-people, seldom if ever, won that battle.

So, it was with great reluctance that I switched camps temporarily and drove to work on the odd day where the weather was particularly inclement. The rest of the time I would walk along the riverside path adjacent to the marina, through an idyllic park to a small pedestrian bridge. Once crossed, the beauty and serenity of my 'cabin at the lake' would be quickly replaced with the din of a sprawling industrial zone. Although this zone was once an extension of vital marine wetlands, I was aware too, of the irony, as I would make my way towards the bus stop, that this was my ticket to drive-free, stress-free commuting.

But very soon that would all change.

The Handi-Dart people informed me that my location, the marina, was out of their serving area so consequently I would have to "find my way to the nearest pick-up point." What this really meant was that I would have to face the overwhelming task of somehow managing to keep an appointment, which would require me to go out in public, catch a bus, and then coordinate a connection with the Handi-dart. How would I be able to pull that off? I thought.

I didn't plan, planning was impossible. I couldn't anticipate, so how could I create a workable system of action? I couldn't, so I didn't. The alarm, if properly set, would sound and I would gradually and groggily get out of bed. Mary made sure I was up, but to get the appointment on time, was up to me. I never remembered the purpose of getting up and appointments, no matter how important, didn't yet exist in my thoughts. Every day was the same, free from expectation or commitment; I would get up and make a cup of tea then sit facing a window, so I could watch the sunrise and its mirror image reflected in the river. What else was there 'to do'? Nothing, I was unaware of time limits, deadlines, no urgent matters to tend to. I would just *be*.

But to *just be* required at least a minimal level of body/mind cognizance, which I didn't yet possess so no, that wasn't accurate so *what* was this state and *where* was the I in there? I wasn't yet sure of any of that stuff.

Somehow, though I did manage to get to the bus stop, get on, pay and get off at the right place-most of the time. Those rides were terror-filled experiences which sounds overly dramatic now, but believe me the fear was very real to me at the time. The bus scene would play out as a slow but predictable unravelling of sorts given my emotional start point, which was always very fragile.

I no longer knew how to count money or what the denominations meant. Money whether coin or paper, when in the palm of my hands felt and looked like foreign matter. Putting together a bus fare was a job of gargantuan proportions.

I would usually sit in the courtesy seats, because my sense of balance was haywire, and being prone to falling over, made standing laughable. I would practically lunge toward these first few rows of seats, so as to get my body planted onto something stable. Then the problem of remembering why I caught the bus in the first place would arise, and it would take some time to sort out the question which seemed to be more like an unsolvable mystery.

The challenges would just keep coming. Where do I get off? How do I get off the bus? I had to watch others first, then only after observing several people had I reasoned that I would need to pull the cord, which ran past my head, which would then turn on the green light indicating someone was getting off. That was the *how?* And next was the *where?* Most days I undershot the correct stop due to an ever increasing fear of passing by the right one, or alternatively would sleep right through my stop. If I remembered to, I prepared myself for the next step which was to get up and as quickly as possible get to an upright bar and hang on. Relief only came once I stepped off and could rest, unaware of the next step which soon would require my full attention.

This anxiety riddled routine was to be repeated many, many more times over the course of the next 6 months with only minor variation.

Fatigue Is For Normal People; Exhaustion Is The Realm Of The Brain Injured.

Resting became a constant. During the next weeks and months at the rehab centre, I would be permitted to lay down, as resting was not only encouraged, but promoted as a compulsory behaviour for healing the brain. They, the staff, just seemed to understand what I needed without any explanation from me which was fortunate, as this ultimately led to some stress-reduction.

According to my neighbors at the marina I had been sleeping 23 hours a day. They reasoned this because I came out of my boat only for brief moments each day looking as if I had just woken up yet, I'd complain of feeling exhausted. Several friends insisted they had been knocking at my door at regular intervals wondering all the while if I were okay. Then there was the food, laid out hours before, still outside my door uneaten & untouched. No amount of sleep seemed to change my overall demeanor which was exhaustion.

I looked unkempt and felt completely haggard.

When I showered it was at the instruction of someone else, because that would never have occurred to me. Once in the shower, there was the challenge of figuring out what the taps were meant for. I would ask myself "What do I do in here? What am I doing in here"? I'd shampoo my hair but would forget to rinse, and then leave the house dressed in whatever clothing was nearby. Not until I'd gotten to the bus stop would I then realize that it was pouring rain. I'd arrive there soaking wet with no way of drying off and vaguely aware that streaks of shampoo were cascading down my arms and legs. Like most things though, this too would be quickly forgotten, unless someone pointed it out, I would simply carry on my way oblivious.

…Back to the exhaustion though…sleeping or more accurately, attempting to sleep consumed most of my day then, and even now at times, it continues to be a challenge. Is there anything more disruptive to one's life as lack of or just poor quality of sleep? I don't think so, whatever the reasons might be.

I understand now that an injured brain requires immense amounts of downtime. The oft repeated statement "learn to pace yourself" comes to mind, but at that time it was a concept which eluded my comprehension like most other concepts. I didn't get it, and wouldn't get it for a decade or more. It was an idea for someone like me who used to marvel at the amount of productivity I could generate that, in my damaged state, seemed foreign, yet I now recognise that pacing oneself was precisely how I had managed to be so productive in my former life.

I'm OK You Are Not!

I had been keeping regular appointments at the rehab centre with the Neuropsychiatric member of my rehab team who had encouraged me to also participate in their in-house group therapy. I'd go but even before the end of the first session I knew, or so I thought, that I didn't belong there. The other patients seemed highly dysfunctional and most sessions, which lasted about an hour, were taken up with stories detailing, in my opinion, drinking and drug problems. By then I had been clean & sober for over a decade and so didn't consider 'those people' appropriate peers. Week after week, I was somehow convinced to keep attending the group sessions, but I had protested constantly. I'd realize later that I wasn't able to see myself as disabled then, and that this disconnection to my reality created conflict. I didn't yet embrace the idea that I was brain injured; I was still 'fine' despite the ever mounting stacks of evidence to the contrary.

After 4 or 5 group sessions, I remembered sharing briefly about my personal progress. The reactions from the others were so emphatically positive; everyone, all 5 or 6 of them praised me for speaking for the first time and for appearing to be getting better i.e. not sleeping through 95% of the session!

Right after that, for a fleeting instance it crossed my mind that it was possible that I wasn't really, mentally following what was *actually* happening around me.

Can't Handle Anything Anymore

At the same time there were other dramas being played out in my personal life with friends. There were two people in particular whose breakup continually spilled into my life and caused me great stress and naturally, anxiety. I would end most of those phone calls with tears and pleads to please stop calling me, until eventually I'd asked them both to just not call me anymore. I'd felt a kind of desperation in trying to get away from the relentless feelings of apprehension, and it became clear that I could no longer deal with even the most minor of adversities, so I'd begged them to stop calling altogether, which unfortunately only served to further isolate me.

To experience myself losing it over what used to qualify as simple 'don't get bent out of shape' type situations was really tough. I didn't recognise myself anymore and I wasn't behaving like the person I knew to be me. My speech was slow and chopped up, plus I'd feel and look pained, when attempting with great effort to form a complete sentence.

Something my therapist said to me once really stuck inside my brain somewhere. When referring to my new self I'd often exclaim "that's not me or this isn't like me"! One day she casually asked, "if not you, then who?", "who is this 'other' you keep referring to?" I was at first stumped then horrified. It *was* me after all.

More Rehab

Other rehab team members consisted of Physiotherapists, to address my other physical injuries and an Occupational Therapist to help me sort out the mounting and neglected pile of legal papers from my employer, union and lawyer.

If you are or someone you know is on this journey alone, and if you haven't already, you could find yourself eventually falling through the gaping cracks in what is commonly called the 'system'. It's almost impossible not to. I had a 'Team' and I didn't know then how fortunate I was but the sentiment, "you are so lucky" was to become yet another recurrent theme on my journey to self-reclamation and self-reinvention.

Brain injury renders us incapable of self-advocacy especially during those first few weeks, months or years post injury, and for countless others, not ever. Some people do carry over the remnants of certain skills and abilities into their new existence but many others never had such competences to begin with. Those people start with nothing. Their slates wiped clean but not to be confused with a fresh start; a blank canvass is great if you're a painter, if you're brain injured, it's a dreadful predicament.

The Walking Wounded

The first time I heard this phrase, I mean really *heard* it was when it became the mantra of my new culture. Radha, from GF Strong introduced me to my new self this way. She was always so encouraging and her belief and confidence in my recovery did eventually rub off on me.

For a while post-accident, I was just confused which then gave way in part to anxiety, which subsequently mutated into a kind of victim mentality. I had somehow been wronged and was paying the high price for it; for someone else's mistake. Fortunately for me, though being brain injured meant this new mental reality didn't last, and soon another more relevant one would replace it. This concept too was repeated to me many times while in Rehab. Nothing, not your thoughts, your beliefs or your understanding is static, it will change. Who you think you are now will not be true in a week or a month, and you will need to find a way to adapt and make adjustments to your ever-changing inner world, if you want to get better.

I think what it meant to me was that while I experienced my world as altered, most people on the outside didn't. If you didn't know me before you would have thought nothing of my behaviour. However, I knew I was different, and my close friends, certain family members and others from my numerous social circles knew this truth too. They could tell and would often comment "you are not all right or you're not all there anymore" followed by "are you getting the right kind of help?" and "what is your doctor doing about it?" Answering to them was not so easy but their message was clear; they knew that I was not OK and I knew it too.

You Look Fine

It's natural to assume I suppose that if I *look* fine then I must *be* fine.

I'd probably operated from this level for much of my previous life. I know that I'd judged people, and at times very harshly for their presumed wrongs. If I'd noticed someone taking up the handicap parking space I would observe them for a minute or two to be sure in my own mind that they deserved to use that sacred and privileged space. If they exited their vehicle with ease then I'd wait to see if the obligatory cane or crutches or the indisputable, universal symbol for disability, the wheelchair would materialize. If one of my definitions were met then I would carry on with my business satisfied that everything was right and proper. It was that simple and that obvious. What more could anyone possibly have to add?

Clearly, now, there is plenty more.

My perceived appearance became a constant reminder of the facts. I say perceived because I had not been aware of my refection in any mirror for some time. I don't recall seeing anything reflected back whenever I did look. I didn't react nor feel disturbed by this, I just wasn't there. This strangeness about everything, *just was*.

Those words though, "you look fine", disturbed and felt critical to me. What did that mean?

The biggest challenge with this assumption for anyone in this position is to continue to improve and believe that you are not *just crazy* or *just depressed* or *just lazy* or a combination of all the above. I wasn't just fine but I really wanted to be. I'd just wanted to get back to something resembling my former self, so whatever it was going to take to be me again, I'd sign up for it.

In rehab, there were a team of people looking after my physical, emotional and mental needs. There was access to certain resources like people and books and the countless new coping strategies to take in and sort through. There were assessments and reassessments until eventually it was time for me to leave. My program of recovery had been extended by several weeks but still the prospect of leaving really scared me.

My self-belief was at an all-time low. I'd been grappling with a new identity and not really understanding what it all meant. Would I ever work again? Would I ever be OK? I had dreams that needed attention and goals to achieve; I had a life that was waiting for me and any day now, I'd thought then, I would wake up and *be back*; but nothing could be further from reality.

Michelle, the person I knew to be me, was gone forever, but I just didn't believe it yet.

CHAPTER III- PEOPLE *MORE* LIKE ME

September 2002-February 2003

"If you find yourself living in limbo, look for others who perceive themselves to be in the same place and start a *limbo club*"...From-*Objects in the mirror are closer than they appear, by Sol Mongerman*

Before leaving GF Strong for good, I was introduced to several interesting books written by BI survivors. The very first one titled, *Over My Head, A Doctor's Story,* by Claudia Olsen. Her words were my first real introduction to others like me. I wasn't a Doctor nor did I possess a degree like she did but I did consider myself to be a professional in my field of employment and now, like her, I was brain injured.

I did relate in part to her story that gave me a start-line, a relating point, to another person. Incredibly though, I was privately ruthless in my critique of her writing style and promised myself then, that if I *were* ever to write a book, it would be both stylish and entertaining! The thought of this now just makes me laugh out loud, considering that I'd neither written anything nor even had plans to!

The second book I had read was Sol Mongerman's, quoted above. This book was more a practical guide combined with his personal story of becoming brain injured. Plus, he was a Registered Clinical Counselor living and practicing in British Columbia, where I was living at the time of my accident, so I related to his experience on many more levels.

Something that Radha had said to me really stuck. I didn't question why then, but a seed was planted regardless of my knowing it or not. She suggested that I should attend the upcoming Pacific Coast Brain Injury Conference in September. I didn't think much of the idea then and thought I would much rather spend my limited energy resources getting well and getting back to work. That was my real focus.

I had already known how to do the hard work of rehab. My prior life was marked by chapters of injury and illness which required dedication to getting better so I'd become good at it. I just kept going; doing whatever it took, all the while believing that total recovery was imminent. Therefore, the current episode of injury to me was no different and I would be just fine, eventually.

Just before leaving my rehab program, once again, Radha suggested the conference but with the caveat, "you never know Michelle, one day *you* could be up there speaking about your story. You could do that if you wanted too". The idea was crazy but I would never forget it. The idea that I could help others, that's what intrigued and motivated me to get well even more, it was something to grasp towards.

So I went and as fate would have it, I got to meet Sol Mongerman and he was adorable, I think. I tried my best to thank him as he autographed my copy of his book but all that came out at the time was babble. I can only hope he got the message behind all the babbling!

The biggest realization that I'd take away from the conference was that I wasn't alone. I hadn't felt that way in the group at GF Strong and as kind as these, equivalent walking wounded souls were, I couldn't relate to them and in particular, their stories.

The most profound moment at the conference came during a talk by CFL legend, Terry Evanshen, whose own brain injury story is poignantly (and graphically) chronicled in the movie *The Man Who Lost Himself.*

The seminal moment came during the subsequent Q & A session, post talk. A young man, seated at the same table as me a few feet away, stood up and asked his question, his voice shaking. I had thought to myself, how brave he was, and that I would be way too scared to speak up then, and to some degree, now.

Terry had just finished describing how we, in order to continue to recover our lives, needed to keep resisting our urge to hide in ourselves; that the way through our trauma was to keep trying to express ourselves, even when we felt absolutely no connection to the feelings we were attempting to express. In response to this the young man asked simply, "how?!" He then proceeded to describe his feelings of frustration and anguish whenever he tried to express his feelings to his wife about how much he loved her. His problem was that he couldn't connect to those feelings anymore; he could only speak from their place in his memory, *imagining,* how he *used* to feel. I started to cry, the emotion just burst out of me. I swallowed it down and wiped my eyes, *not here,* I had thought then, *please not here.*

The auditorium filled with all those people seemed totally caught up in the moment. We could all relate to this person, his suffering was our suffering.

Terry said nothing. He walked towards the man; arms outstretched, and took him into the safety of his embrace. He hugged the young man emphatically, in silence, then released his grasp with the words, "that's how," simultaneously, a gigantic cauldron of grief bubbled up and boiled inside me; some early indications of things to come.

That happened over 10 years ago but the tears still come whenever I reflect back on it, like now.

"Get Yourself To A Therapy Group"

My time at GF Strong came to its inevitable end and reluctantly I'd moved on with much encouragement from the many caring people there.

It was recommended to me that I should participate in an ongoing 10 - 12 week Trauma Recovery Group facilitated by a brilliant and, in my experience, the most empathetic and kind professional I've ever met; J. Lynne Mann, M, R Psych.

I didn't know what to expect out of a group setting. I mean, in some vague way I'd considered myself a team player but, my jobs were mostly about individual effort and to a lesser degree about the group as a whole. Also for some unknown reason, I had deep feelings of trepidation associated with groups, especially those which formed into circles.

I'd decided to defer to the people who had gotten me this far and joined the weekly gathering of the Trauma Recovery Group or TRG.

The TRG became my new social, emotional, mental and spiritual life-raft.

All the things which I had left behind; social groups, team sports and other outdoor activities, employment, dreams and aspirations, spiritual/mental/emotional/physical self-identities and all the pain resulting, inevitably, from pile upon pile of hurt from these loses, was soon replaced by the solidarity, empathy and safety which operated within the structure of the group. TRG was *that* important to me.

Admittedly though, I barely remember anything from the first 10 or 12 weeks meaning the entire first segment. These segments or blocks of weekly meetings operated on a continual basis for 10 - 12 weeks then, sometime later after that, the next block would commence. The in-group literature consisted of a manual comprised of simple and easy-to-follow pictures and/or graphs; no long paragraphs or complex descriptors or instructions, just back-to-basics stuff. A long, long way from where I *had* been in my former life.

Of course I wasn't really conscious of any of that stuff until I'd become aware enough and present enough, to notice that there *was* a manual. I'd slept, or semi-slept my way through that first block of meetings so the details during that time are sketchy at best. I'd recall several people referring to their sobriety though. I was still sober, so I think this aspect of their stories interested me in some vague way.

As the meetings progressed I'd begin the very, very slow process of waking up to my surroundings, to the point where I would actually participate by sharing something of myself, if only a word or two. Gradually, I would not only share but listen too. I'd begun to notice certain people's faces; they now looked familiar to me. Up until then everyone else's face, including most of my friends were not immediately recognizable. I'd sometimes think, "I should know this person, shouldn't I?'

Another strange facet of BI came into being around that time. I'd believed that I *knew everyone* and that I had some connection to them and that they, everyone including strangers, were known to me somehow. This odd view of the world stayed with me for a long, long time and would repeatedly shift back and forth with the idea that *no one* was recognizable. When I was in the *knowing everyone* phase, social situations were especially pleasant. Alternatively, those periods of *not knowing anyone,* were particularity stressful. And so my view of other people persisted like this for years.

The Disappearance Of The Social-Self

Having a brain injury gifted to me, firstly the existence of, then the understanding of, and lastly the subtle intricacies of *social cues.* I'm referring to the nuances which exist in everyday conversation such as give and take, or to put it another way, talk then listen then be *cued* or prompted to speak again. This subtle but generally unspoken ritual is a process which most people take for granted. I know I used to.

Before brain injury, talking was something I'd just feel in a comfort zone, while doing something, and I wouldn't have to think about it. Words, in all their endless forms, were there when called upon; the wit, the charm, the intelligence all there in one neat and continuous package; in other words-The unbroken *stream of consciousness*.

...but that was then...

With my new self however, conversations, when taking part in a one-to-one situation, it would become painfully obvious to the other person that I'd become completely oblivious to any social cues. There were no nods in agreement or of acknowledgment. My eyes wouldn't stay focused on theirs, but instead, they darted around or looked down avoiding all contact whatsoever. I couldn't concentrate on the words they were speaking long enough to derive their meaning, much less any gist of the totality of the conversation.

The worst moment would come when the cue had been given that the end was near. The speaking part was done and so too the listening. It was time to go, but I didn't get it. I would stand around looking and waiting for something but not knowing what that *something* was. Not understanding that the conversation had run its course. The signals had been given and what remained was to just leave. Usually the other person would say their goodbyes then leave me standing on the spot, dumbfounded, looking like the proverbial deer in the headlights.

I used to characterize it this way. I'm like an alien, new to this planet. I didn't know the language, the customs, food, traditions, idiosyncrasies of behaviour, weather patterns, political systems, units of measure, creatures etc., etc. So, other than my physical appearance, clearly, I just didn't belong here.

Back to my earlier bridge example, imagine, once again that you are standing at the end of a road looking out over a vast chasm to the other side where the road continues on. This space in between was once spanned by a connecting bridge but the bridge is now gone. The way to get to the other side, to continue on the road, is the similar journey one's thoughts take when accessing and then retrieving information from the brain. Like neurons which continually fire together, and then stick together, they form a physical 'bridge' within our brain.

With brain-injury the well-worn paths to the information is no more, yet, we continue to wait for the information to be retrieved because we know it's there. We are stumped, and so look blank or stunned during these endless moments of delay.

But the information never comes, so we try another route or another path but find nothing because there no reliable, existing paths left to follow and all other roads are simply just dead-ends.

I would feel embarrassed by the growing frequency & length of pauses between words whenever I spoke, and this led to the deeper inner-belief, that I was now somehow flawed and unintelligent.

A great deal of my own self-worth and self-esteem I'd perceived about myself was derived from the ability to communicate with others in a concise, intelligent and articulate manner. I'd associated these abilities with my charisma, charm and naturally, my likability. The undoing, the stripping-down of me occurred like this on many countless levels.

Conversing with others was then viewed as a painful, trauma- inducing situation, which was best avoided. Why would anyone wish to continually put themselves in that situation? I didn't, so I preferred instead to take those kinds of risks within the safety of the TRG.

Memory-Gaps

For me the concept, we call *time*, no longer existed. One day led to the next and then the next, indistinct from one another. Months passed in this way, sometimes 3-6 months before I gave it any notice.

I once heard a story told in an AA meeting where this person had had a blackout lasting 6 months. "Wow, that's unreal!" I'd thought at the time, but now I'd experienced similar situations where I'd recollect only vague and fog-like feelings, but not memories of events, persons, places or things.

These episodes of not knowing what had proceeded, the present moment were extremely scary at the time like waking up from a deep sleep, with no recollection of your life prior to that moment. I often said then that it's not like a 'Zen moment', but rather a distracted one.

In a few more years, I would try to put the events of my life back into chronological order. I had memories, but without their corresponding context, but more about that stuff later.

When Ignorance Isn't Bliss

About six months post-accident a strange phenomenon, I'd later refer to as 'The White-Light' experience, descended upon my awareness. It manifested as lightness in mind and body, such as having an odd sense of brightness around me at all times. Often I'd remark about how the weather was beautiful all the time, and I'd become convinced that it was always sunny outside. While my senses remained shut-down or dulled I'd experience my field of vision as though there was a brightly lit bulb overhead, but paradoxically at the same time, unclear and in monochrome, preventing me from perceiving the details of my outer world. Variations of color or distinctions of shape and size instead, appeared as moving or stationary grey blobs.

For a while life felt okay, but more than okay, it was light; not heavy or difficult. This 'white-light' period lasted for about eight months at its most intense then softened into the background of my awareness becoming less and less prevalent as the months passed. I think then that perhaps I was going to be okay, because I was happy-ish, light in attitude and hopeful.

It was during this same period where I had one of those 3-6 month memory gaps. It started in mid-October right after the end of my first stint in the TRG and lasted until sometime in February of the following year.

Friends have filled in some of the blanks, but other than these few snippets of information, I don't remember a thing during these gaps of memory.

I remembered that Mary and I had bought a condominium in a nearby neighborhood, and were scheduled to move in, sometime in March. I'd experienced severe distress and anxiety about leaving the marina and my 'family' there. It was going to be my first move to organise as a brain injured person, but if you knew me as well as some people did, this wouldn't be cause for concern. I had moved house at least 23 times previously. This made me a pro at organising, sorting, and packing and un-packing and naturally, I'd had a talent for delegating tasks to others. However, the memory of me doing things efficiently and with precision did not help in the process this time, and unfortunately the memories didn't match up with the reality. This move would be a personal disaster. I was completely out of sorts this time around; not enough boxes, nothing in the right box, not enough packing tape, insufficient bubble-wrap, things spread all over the boat, and not knowing where to put them. It was complete chaos.

Who I'd been was the person people could count on. I had been the planner, the motivator, the delegator and if necessary, the doer. One way or another I got things done but that was *then* and this is *now,* so consequently the move was extremely stressful for everyone in its sphere of influence; my neighbors, their friends, Mary, my cats and me.

CHAPTER IV-FALSE START #1

March 2003-August 2003

"In the process of recovering from a brain injury a false start is evidence that you are rebuilding yourself and you just haven't found the right path yet"....Objects in the Mirror are closer than they appear.

Sometime during the haze of the 'white light' experience, I'd managed to take a trip to Hawaii with Mary. I've seen a few pictures so I know that it happened but my memories of them seem surreal and dream- like. Driving the Hana highway and eating fresh pineapple and not being able to stand up on a surfboard anymore, all real but without the emotion attached or any other anchoring details

I really think that the problem lies with my memories being out of chronological order. What this means is that I have memories of events, but do not know *when* they happened or *where* they fit. I've nothing to attach them to, thus they lack their corresponding context.

We Can Do This!

Before Mary and I moved into our new (it was new to us) condo, it needed some, well actually a lot of work, before it was fit to be occupied. So, soon after emerging from my most recent White Out, we got to work with the planning, preparing, the delegating and the doing. All of this effort was soon followed by that earlier painful move, but that was to come on the heels of the renovation.

I believed I was a master organizer and commenced the work of planning out the renovation, something I'd never done before. My confidence as an over achiever had convinced me that I could do it, without assistance, on time and on budget.

We, Mary and I, had roughly six weeks or so to make the transformation, and bring our new abode into the 21st century.

The carpets were '70's' shag impregnated with 30+ years of cigarette smoke and ash. The walls had an ashen hue like the complexion of its former occupants; yellow-streaked with patches of mottled gray. Absolutely gross!

I do remember, with clarity, the smell that was similar to the dumpster stench, which had been shadowing my every in-breath for a while by then. Only this smell had the added complexity of cigarettes and something else which I'd never quite get a handle on. It didn't matter I reasoned, it was all going to ripped out by some as yet unknown persons.

It had an amazing patio, 10x20 feet of luxurious privacy; this was the real heart of the place. The kitchen, which, in the past was usually my favorite place to conjure up new recipes and concoctions was not so inviting. It was a dead-end for a room with only one way in and the same way out. I didn't like to go in there for any length of time. The lighting was nothing short of horrid; a dreadful four-panel recessed fluorescent dinosaur.

It had one big bedroom which faced out overlooking the glorious patio and beyond that the fenced-in common-area that marked the border of the entire property. The bathroom was okay, but the tub and toilet needed addressing. So to recap; the entire suite required a total make-over; new paint, new floors, new or refinished tub, new toilet, new countertops and backsplashes (kitchen & bathroom), new kitchen and miscellaneous lighting, new moulding, new fridge, stove and dishwasher, new washer & dryer, new window coverings and new closet doors.

Mentally my standards were intact, but my income no longer reflected my ability to procure the things which matched up to those tastes. Soon after my accident I'd qualified, through my employer, for short-term disability this meant that my wages would be halved. Following that, unless, or until I was deemed permanently disabled, my employers' insurance company would then take over and manage my income and rehabilitation.

My union contributed a few hundred dollars towards my overall income each month, that helped off-set the shortfall. I had opted-in to the union disability plan a few years before my injury, and could not have predicted the need for it would become so great. At the time I felt stressed and hard done by, but in retrospect I could not have been more fortunate!

But, back to the Reno!

I'd ignored the obvious; I wasn't organised, comprehended little, was easily and regularly confused, could not track my spending, had very little money, was incapable of tracking or comprehending a time-line, often felt nauseous, slept most of the time, had no energy to even walk our newly adopted dog, Sally, couldn't construct or conceptualize a meal but most troubling of all, I could not recognise or verbalize any of these deficits. So consequently, I'd convinced myself that I was just fine!

The Beginning And The End

The work began a *little* behind schedule. I had organised all the appropriate tradespeople and, I imagined in my own mind, that being one myself had given me a unique understanding and perspective of what exactly was required to transform our dungeon into the castle; it all seemed to make complete sense, at least in theory. I had done some minor work on a house project some years before, but this was on a whole different scale, but those details did not discourage me however. I alone had coordinated all the work much like a foreman or general contractor might, so I alone was left to explain the many discrepancies of time, money and miscellaneous other conflicts, which inevitably surfaced.

The work and subsequent chaos carried on for weeks.

There were many, many hiccups and since I had positioned myself as the go-to person for any and all problems, which were endless, and never quite completely resolved, I was infinitely more stressed than everyone else, I thought. I would feel terribly underappreciated and unfairly criticized, causing Mary and I to argue constantly. Bad feelings permeated the space which was supposed to represent a fresh start, the new beginning to our life together.

After one particularly nasty exchange, I knew then that I'd need to move on, and decided right at that moment, I would soon need to be on my own. The idea seemed crazy because clearly I couldn't manage my life, yet I had to try. The people at GF Strong had encouraged me the previous summer to move in with Mary. They understood the challenges I'd faced on my own, but now after nearly 9 months of co-habitation, previously on my rented boat home, and now in this new space, the prospects of continuing with this situation, was too much for me. I'd come to the realization that I'd have to leave and face my overwhelming fear of having to take care of myself.

Recovering From A False Start

Once the renovation and renewing stopped, (notice I didn't write completed), I knew I needed to get rest, so I took a few months to basically just sleep, and I would also need to lay down in between naps. I still never felt sufficiently rested ever, but the reality was what it was. I had to go, and determined that by early July, I'd need to start the process of finding a new place to live.

Mary worked full-time this allowed me to rest all day, but eventually I'd need to just get out and get to the dreaded task of apartment hunting.

In time, I was able to walk the dog, first just to the end of the block and back, which was simply exhausting. Eventually, I was able to take a full walk around the block. This routine very, very slowly graduated into several blocks. The entire walk not lasting for more than 15 or 20 minutes and ending with me looking and feeling totally haggard.

Over time, I was able to write down information from the many 'For Rent' notices, posted along my dog-walking routes. This led to me finding a lovely 1 bedroom, rustic-looking suite in a converted heritage home just a few blocks from my current apartment. I hadn't yet fully unpacked, but that didn't make things any easier second time around. Mary assisted me with the move, but those days were filled with awkwardness and unspoken rage. Mary was beside herself, and I don't think she really believed I would carry through with my plans to leave. It was an awful time for both of us, but in particular for Mary. I'd left her with the full-time responsibility of caring for a dog and a home, with her dream life of happy-ever-after, being totally shattered.

For a brief time afterwards, I continued to walk Sally, while Mary was at work. When or how this routine ended, I don't remember, but eventually it did with Mary taking over the full-time care of Sally.

Now all I had on my plate was me and that was terrifying!

CHAPTER V- LEARNING TO EXIST

August 2003-March 2004

"Course correction can be effectively used as a metaphor for any progressive action you are undertaking"...Objects in the mirror are closer than they appear.

Moving on sounded good at the time, but in reality everything about it frightened me. Without the support of my friends, I doubt that I would have been able to take the leap of faith required to do so.

The irony is that my new home had everything that I'd require to begin the life-long process of healing. My suite was located on the second floor of a two-story converted house. There were only four suites, which meant six people in total, including me, lived there. It had a lovely outside deck overlooking the covered parking area, and beyond that several enormous and beautiful evergreen trees.

The parking, laundry and storage facilities were all included in the rent, it was affordable and perfect in every other way too. My transformation from existing in a fog of uncertainty and confusion, could now progress into existing with purpose and intermittent fog, which *was* better than the alternative.

You Are Officially, A *Disabled* Person

Just a few months prior, I was deemed *permanently disabled* by the federal government disability department.

It was mandated by my union the previous year that, persons like me, who were on temporary disability for a specific time period, were required to apply for permanent disability status from the government. I'd been going through the out-patient program at GF Strong at the time. The paperwork had come in the mail, but I had felt completely overwhelmed by it, until it too, was quickly forgotten. Luckily for me, I had good friends watching over some of my more pressing affairs.

My friend, Sheila, would often ask me all the right questions, but I never had any answers. To say that I had a grasp on anything would have been a stretch of the imagination. For a time too, Mary would occasionally accompany me to appointments, filling in all the gaping holes in my memory. I was also lucky to have my neighbors donating their time and energy as a taxi-service, as well as a meals-on-wheels provision.

These people, and many others, contributed enormously to my well-being and, although during much of that time their kind deeds went unnoticed and unappreciated, they continued to care for and watch over me. Yes, I was very lucky indeed!

Getting this new identity of being disabled, a label given to me from someone outside of me, took a measure of time to sink in.

I had really thought though, 'but I'm not like those other disabled types. How can I be considered disabled?"

I was in a classic catch-22 situation. On the one hand, I'd refused to pin the disabled sign on my back, yet paradoxically, I *was* disabled, just one more of my life's many ironies.

I tried to absorb the new idea of being a disabled person, but my body and mind rejected it completely, like some gigantic spoon filled with Buckley's cough syrup. It repulsed me, and it tasted awful. I couldn't even say the word to myself, much less out loud to an empty room. Not even to my cats!

Yes, I had multiple problems. Physically, I was a mess, so too emotionally and mentally, but spiritually however, things were much worse than even that word could describe. To call my spiritual state as being disabled, well ok, it was disabled, but the damage I'd felt inside could be compared to an apocalyptic wasteland. I didn't just *feel* destroyed and empty, I *was* those things; my inner world *was* a wasteland.

False Start #2

Around October 2003, I made the decision that I would not become my label. I'd settled in to my new place and my new neighbors. This was the beginning of a quiet but brief time of self-examination, plus another segment of TRG meetings had just begun.

The Trauma Recovery Group once again became my focus. The meetings had been moved to a new, quieter location. They were being held in a church located a few blocks from my new apartment. I had re-qualified for my driver's license, so I chose to drive to the meeting at first, and a while later, I opted to walk when I felt able to.

A greater awareness of myself and my environment allowed me to share more of these realizations with the group. For the first time since my accident, I'd sensed inside my being, the activation of several emotional states, such as intimacy with others and a bit of joy too.

I had begun to open up and bond with individuals, and not just the group as a whole. I was beginning to feel a little better inside. Here was a safe place where I was understood. I didn't need to stress about finding the words or constructing a sentence that made sense. I could, if only just for that 2 hour block once per week, be okay. It was something to build on.

In my new (and previous) life, feeling even a bit better meant it was time to start another project! I'd made the decision to get back to the gym by reactivating a long forgotten lifetime membership to a local outfit. What could be easier? The process of trying to organise my gear was demoralizing. I had inexplicably gained weight since becoming injured, and until then, I was unaware that I'd become heavier, and could not account for how that could have happened. I needed new work out garb first, and during the ensuing search through my copious amounts of clothes, I came across my long forgotten bike riding shorts. My initial reaction was to feel frozen with fear, then as that thought melted into the void a new, better plan emerged. Perhaps, I could ride my bike to the gym and that way I could forgo the cardio machines, which intimidated me anyway. This way, I could start with stretching and then move on to the weights!

The plan was obviously all wrong, but I'd stick to it anyway and after much delay my gear was eventually organized, and so was I.

Over the course of the next few days there were several, terrifying failed attempts to get back to my former life such as riding my bike again, and navigating the traffic. Eventually, I'd recover from them and simply drive to the gym, my bike back in its proper place in the storage locker.

During the period immediately after the accident, and while I was still living on the boat, I had my bike repaired. I had made inquiries to many bike shops before someone agreed to repair it, rather that throw it away. My bike was a symbol of me; a mental imprint of who I'd thought I was, and I could not let it go. I kept all the bent and broken pieces too until eventually, years later, I allowed myself to throw them away.

In an earlier moment of despair though, I had thrown out my helmet. It had a huge crack on it, plus the foam was caved in at the place where my head impacted the hood and windshield of the car. Best get a new one, I thought so that's what I did.

Once at the gym I'd really believed that my former workout routine would simply kick-in, I could presumably slide right into it as if nothing had happened, and in so doing reclaim the exhilaration one feels with being fit. Since I hadn't ridden my bike, I'd have to confront the dreaded cardio machines. This brought up many fears like using electronics, regardless of their simplicity, the frequent random sensation of things moving under me, falling down-forwards or backwards but the most dreaded of all, looking like a complete idiot.

Asking for help wasn't an option because I wasn't capable of following a conversation, so I couldn't get the information I needed, and I couldn't be sure exactly how to structure the question. So I'd just persevere on my own.

Eventually over the course of several weeks and months, I did manage to get a workout plan in place. I would just avoid certain treadmills because I was convinced they were defective and was never able to get them moving. Instead, I would wait for the one that I knew I could get to start, but sometimes this meant I would have to wait around for a while. Doing this had its own built-in pitfalls, as I would inevitably forget what I was doing there, and eventually looking as casual as was possible, I'd simply wander over to the stretching area.

My new weight-lifting experience was nothing like the old one. My muscles didn't respond the way I remembered nor did they have any measure of strength and I'd feel weak all over. At first this was very discouraging, but eventually over time I adjusted by lowering my expectations and the weight. Despite the effort, exercise was not feeling like the fun times I imagined in the months prior when I was getting myself organised enough to come back. It just felt awful, now.

This experience was different from those first few months post injury, when my mental awareness was disconnected from my body. At that time, my arms would just hang by my sides and my limbs appeared like foreign matter protruding out in front of me. Back then, my perception of my body was confined to my head, occasionally my legs and feet, and to a lesser degree my neck and shoulders. As time passed, the awareness that I had a body came through showing themselves as the slow, filtered bodily sensations of pain. Those sensations became the primary mental and emotional connections to my body and all of its protrusions. I felt pain, therefore I did exist.

And as this same person working out in the gym, this time around, there was just more pain and more fatigue. Why wasn't this working? Why didn't I feel better? I had put in the time and the effort, but inexplicably, I wasn't getting the payoff.

Why Am I So Tired All Of The Time?!

Previous to my BI, I had worked out habitually for decades, participated in four-season sports, commuting to work by bike, planned regular & frequent hiking trips, and all of this activity tempered with daily meditation and scripture study. I had been busy all the time.

But now, I was exhausted by a watered down gym routine that I had persisted in doing for months. While I did lose some weight and toned up a bit too, there was no elusive payoff. I noticed too that my breathing wasn't the same as I'd remembered either. It was short and rapid like being on the brink of a full-on panic attack, 'when would the ecstasy and the gratification of working out materialize?' I wondered.

It never did, so feeling defeated and deflated, I reluctantly let go of yet another former-life ritual. Another loss, which I'd filed somewhere in my psyche along with the acknowledgement that they were beginning to add up.

I didn't completely stop using weights, as I owned a compact set of free-weights, and continued an abbreviated routine at home. I also walked more frequently for TRG meetings and trips to the grocer. One interesting side note to the workouts was that for the first time since the injury, I noticed my reflection in the mirror. My appearance first startled then frightened me. My face and expression had changed dramatically and seemed like a stranger's face, not mine. I didn't recognise the unfamiliar reflected image. This person was heavier, with an ultra-pale complexion, and she looked terrified. I decided it was best not to look too long.

I focused instead, on just trying to keep going. I wanted to get better, get back to work and back to my life. The life I presumed had been patiently waiting for me to reclaim it.

It's Not Just Fatigue, I'm *Exhausted*!

I was so tired all the time. Exhaustion was my closest companion, (which my cats loved, because they preferred to sleep most days away, and now they had company). That, however, is a subject which could be another book in itself, titled 'The cats that saved my life!'

I believed that no one, except those at the TRG, could really comprehend the level of fatigue I was living with, including the many doctors and specialists I'd seen. It was no fault of theirs. They couldn't possibly grasp the totality of BI without having firsthand knowledge. It was something that they simply didn't have.

The experience of being brain injured, as a 'walking wounded' person, occurs inside of the mind. It's an inner experience with outer consequences. I realise we could make a convincing argument that all life *is* that way, yet those persons who aren't brain injured, would still not grasp my meaning.

I knew I was altered, yet if I needed to convince a stranger of that fact it was going to be a tough challenge. There were times when I was called a fraud, a malingerer, lazy, just depressed, just de-conditioned, just greedy, just something *other* than brain injured. To some of these so-called specialists, the idea that I could be injured was a threat to their firmly held belief systems that were also the foundation of their existence.

What I've come to accept on the subject of the opinion of others regarding who I *might* be and what I *may* be experiencing is this; everyone has an opinion, it may be personal, medical, legal or professional in nature but is fundamentally flawed due to the overriding reality that it belongs to them, hence, is removed from me. It is their *observation* of me but is *not* me.

Expressed another way, as the scientific certainty that it is; '*the thing* (me) *that is being observed, is changed due to the act of observation by the observer* (everyone else)' - Quantum Physics 101.

Okay, Back To The Exhaustion...

Feeling tired all the time, like all other brain injury symptoms required some adjustment time and a blueprint for success, in other words, a plan and a project!

To be away from home, specifically my sofa or bed, for more than an hour at a time meant a plan of *inaction* would be necessary.

The first part of my new plan required changing the back-seating zone in my car. The seats came down and would suffice as a somewhat cozy bed. It was flat, so it would do. I loaded up the car with blankets and pillows, plus the tinted windows provided adequate privacy, not that I cared about that at the time. When the moment came where mandatory rest or sleep was imminent, privacy, literally took a back seat.

And so, driving became more restful when I didn't feel so panicked at the prospect of being stranded somewhere in downtown Vancouver, with no bed or place to crash. If friends were at work or somewhere else out of contact/out of range, it wasn't a problem.

Driving & Resting Strategies

I continued to live in the heritage apartment in New Westminster, a small city, about a 25 minute Skytrain ride or 45 minute drive, sometimes longer, into Vancouver. I didn't yet have sufficient confidence to maneuver through the Skytrain hordes, or figure out the honor ticketing system, so I chose instead to avoid it altogether, especially since I'd already identified public transit as a personal safety hazard.

Some good friends, seeing my struggles with exhaustion, gave me spare keys to their homes, so if necessary, I could collapse there and rest at a moment's notice. Soon I had numerous 'crash-pads' setup all along my driving routes, and the subsequent security this provided me was tremendous.

If I was away from my home however, for more than 2 hours, I determined this was when I entered the 'danger zone' of exhaustion. This physical and psychological barrier manifested itself repeatedly and seemingly at the worst possible instances. It was so severe, that even my crash-pad strategy could not cope, and I absolutely had to get back home before crossing this Rubicon.

After being caught in the danger zone enough times to the point where; I could no longer verbally express my needs, appeared 'drunk', felt inebriated, and seem to be just generally incoherent, I was forced to develop a new and better plan. I decided it was time to move... again.

Trying To Make Sense Of My Memories

Fortunately, moving didn't happen right away, which gave me more time to settle down, and get to the business of putting my life back in order. Only this time, it was chronological order. This task became a massive undertaking (one which still goes on today) that served to distract me from my otherwise preoccupation with the idea of moving.

My lawyer had determined that I might benefit from the services of an Occupational Therapist. I simply agreed not knowing what it all meant, then contacted my healthcare professional friends to get an OT pre-visit rundown.

I still didn't understand the purpose of the OT, until she was sitting in my living room with me asking question after question about me. I deferred to memory, which is to say I could really only talk about who I was, only as I remembered myself to be.

At this juncture in post-injury, I was still expecting to wake-up to myself; to snap out of this mind numbing state. I related to this state as a temporary condition, and if I could only just wake-up from it, I'd be fine. The Michelle I knew and who I believed I really was, was still in there somewhere, and if the right amount of time could pass, she would re-emerge; she *had* to.

...okay, back to memory re-construction...

The clearest impression I have of the OT's visit was around

an exercise developed to stimulate one's memories. She suggested we start a 'timeline of events' based on what I could remember, so this timeline would help me make sense of those memories.

She talked while I wrote some things down, and within a few minutes I literally had my life back. I mean, that there were and continue to be huge gaps in my life without the corresponding life description and, obviously I was alive during these rifts of time, but, what was happening then?; what was I doing?; how did I feel?; what was I thinking about? That stuff remained a mystery.

But in that moment, none of that mysterious stuff mattered, because the little piece of paper with just a few things scrawled on it stared back at me and proclaimed "this is your life!" It was so simple which was its underlying brilliance; even I could understand it.

I've since expanded the timeline at regular intervals, and this exercise stimulates my brain to process in a linear thought pattern, which helps me maintain concentration. I can focus only on one thing at a time, in one direction at a time and in single dimension of time, i.e. the here and now. I can now organise my past in this way.

Say for example I was to concentrate fully on the year 1991. Eventually, I remembered something significant, because I quit drinking in June of that year. With this event as a start point, I could then think about what else may have been going on around me during this time. If I tried to remember the whole picture at once, nothing would make sense to me but, if I focused on the event of quitting drinking and moved my attention to what else was going on at that exact time; the people I saw at AA meetings; rehab; the friends who celebrated my sobriety with me; my partner at the time; what I was doing for employment such as specific projects, etc., this worked and stimulated more and more memories.

I thought that *if* I was able of put my life back together this way, then *maybe* I could get the *feelings associated* with the memories back too?

Once I accepted and understood this need of my injured brain, that, order and simplicity stimulated memories, then life did start to get better.

The Beginning Of "The Non-Stop Chatter"

I never really liked talking on the phone for any length of time, especially outside of working hours.

My job involved many hours of telephone interaction with customers, other employees and various outside persons and organisations. While on the phone, I would also be scanning the 'trouble queues' which listed items for immediate action, scouring my many notepads for other details, making mental notes regarding any incoming orders, and various other requests for my time and attention. Sometimes, while I would be caught up in all that, someone, or a line-up of some ones, might be standing next to my desk, needing even more immediate assistance.

I was at everyone's beck-and-call, which was naturally how I liked things in my world because I was good at it and enjoyed being needed. But, when work was done so too was the persona of having to take care of all the problems. I was off-duty, at least until my pager called me back to work, which happened often.

With this in mind, it was very strange behaviour for me to be yakking on the phone to people for hours. Before my injury, my friends and family could never get a hold of me by phone. I was always too busy or too tired of talking to others to be engaged in conversation with them for more than a few minutes at a time and now, I was talking and talking and still more talking. I talked about anything and everything and repeated myself constantly; I was a talking machine!

Notice I didn't say conversationalist, that would imply talking *then* listening, which was not how my version of a conversation went. I did all the nattering while the unfortunate person, or at times persons, who were forced to listen, could not get more than a word or a mere implied word in edgewise.

As the stream of consciousness flowed, I began to feel better about myself. After all, I was *communicating* with others again, which meant I just might belong in the world.

To the poor unfortunates, who were literally stuck on the phone as I blabbed and blabbed well, this was all just part and parcel of their many adjustments to the new me. Something that began to happen that had never happened before, to me, was their eventual attempts to extricate themselves from my incessant talking. This was new. People didn't end conversations with me; I did the ending, the hanging up of the phone first, after all, I was typically the one with nothing more to add or subtract.

Slowly, very slowly, I did start to notice the trend of my calls becoming shorter and shorter as people became much savvier about how best to deal with the my frequent daily phone interruptions to their lives. I can only imagine how difficult this might have been if I were texting and emailing on the same scale. I hadn't yet fully embraced those forms of interaction. Otherwise, those disruptions could have been much worse for everyone.

I didn't feel hurt about it. I don't think I had access to that emotion. I just accepted it, I guess, and moved on to the next person. My brain's capacity to absorb was limited. This could be viewed as a godsend or a burden depending on what the information coming at me was about.

I wanted the capacity to remember, regardless of the content. I now realise that in my brain's arrested state, what it could grasp was that which it could *safely* hang on to. If I had to deal with the mountains of emotion, grief, distress and frustration all at once, or in the moment, the inevitable brain overload would have been disastrous.

If No One Will Talk To Me, I'll Talk To Myself!

Although by now there were now long silent breaks between phone calls, the conversations didn't stop in my head.

In fact, it was even more spirited in there!

My brain would not shut off. The babbling went on and on and I could not interrupt, much less stop the chatter. I tried to get back into meditating just to get a handle all the 'noise', and I'd thought too, to some extent, that I was becoming even more tired from all the nonstop brain activity. It *was* tiring to be the sole participant to all the thought processes and verbalizations.

Meditating used to be a daily practice; breathing in deeply then holding my breath for a brief moment, then, two more repetitions signalled to my brain to commence its descent into quiet reflection. I loved to meditate, because it was as important to me as breathing; it was how I took every breath. With a silent pause, all life around me seemed calm and mostly joy-filled, because I was calm and mostly bliss-filled. My outer life demanded it of me, and so did I.

There *were* difficulties in my former life too, some things easier to get beyond than others. There were previous illnesses demanding attention. Some were chronic, plus work and sports injuries as well. There were also sick time issues, authority figures and shop-stewards to be dealt with. My daily work tasks and responsibilities were in a state of flux. It was the changing times we were in as much as anything else. Corporations were starting to implement their massive downsizing strategies through buy-outs and layoffs, while union-bashing and busting became commonplace. These new employment realities became tolerated and accepted as just part of the big-business stratagem. Many people were worried enough to take employment positions that were beneath their qualifications; soon the nineties would give way to a brave new world-the new millennium.

But I had meditation. I had a way to cope, and so thought that I was handling life better than most.

Maybe I was coping better, it didn't really matter anymore because for years after acquiring the brain injury, I longed for this past-life and despite all of its inherent shortcomings it remained a better alternative to my current new-life situation.

Disconnection From 'The Source'

If you are a person who enjoys meditation and reflection then you probably understand the lead-in above. If you are connected, through whatever your belief system might be, then you understand that God or Source or Creator is there supporting you, guiding you, reassuring you and that you are in service of and for this Energy for the Greater Good (or some version of the above).

This *was* the foundation of my drive; my purpose in life was wrapped around it. I had the confidence and belief that no matter what everything was as it should be in accordance with a Higher Intelligence. I never felt sad or *really* worried because I had an intact connection to Source. I didn't just feel like a channel for love, I believed I was a channel for mostly good things.

When I became injured, I didn't at first grasp the details of the many losses- it took time to digest their absence. When the act of meditating was impossible, almost immediately, I understood the impact to my world would be huge.

I *felt* the disconnection to source like a vast emptiness, and I could no longer sense the familiar presence of bliss or calm, which I'd become accustomed to. It was as if my spiritual routing to source had been somehow cut off, and I was adrift grasping for but finding nothing solid to hang on to. I was lost.

I could see a similarity to my new-self and a PV (photovoltaic) panel; cut off from sunlight (source) and unable to re-charge it would eventually fall into disrepair and be of no use anymore. That was how I felt about myself at the time, as no longer having value in the world.

The Return Of (Select) Emotions

The first experience of feeling an emotion of something other than fear came to me uninvited as hyper-sensitivity to suggestion. In other words, hysteria!

I became ultra-defensive in certain situations, and people close to me would have said that I could be defensive at times anyway, but now, clearly I have graduated! This new expression of grief would catch me completely off-guard coming out of nowhere. I never felt it coming on and it just burst out of me without prior warning rapidly destabilizing my psyche. I felt possessed by unknown and unfriendly entities who created 'episodes' of outbursts, usually in the form of whimpering and panic-stricken rants, which made me even more wary of connecting with strangers.

I remember a trip to the grocery store to get 3 items. I had a list which gave me a little confidence. By then, I had figured out that if I just stayed away from the center isles, I could remain somewhat focused on those 3 (*never* more than 3), articles of necessity. Invariably though, I usually needed to get help to locate my things.

What this meant was asking, out loud for help, except I didn't like the sound of my own voice. It never sounded the way I imagined or remembered it, but it sounded meek and frightened. I couldn't re-connect me to *that* voice.

Usually though someone would find me first, as was often the case, wandering around looking and acting lost. "Can I help you find something?" I'd stand there frozen in place; stammering, searching for the word or groups of words but nothing would come to my rescue, but then occasionally something did come, "help?"

Holding my crumpled list and with hands shaking, I could show it to the stock person without verbalizing. If they started to give directions, then I was once again lost, but increasingly I would get an escort through the labyrinth of grocery products directly to what I came for. My hysterics must have had the power to induce feelings of pity in some, but whatever the real reason I had my 3 items, navigated the check-out (more hysteria) then raced outside to the safety of my car; my refuge. Hallelujah!

These outbursts of mild hysteria became more frequent, but

mercifully they didn't last long before they morphed into something much less dramatic, such as just panic.

Feeling vulnerable was my normal waking state of being. This underlying condition created the panic which would then undermine the stability of practically every situation I was confronted with. It just kicked-in like some automatic gear; no shifting required. I didn't feel it, and wasn't aware of it until there was sufficient stimulation in my world i.e. getting directions from a stranger, going into a store, answering the phone. Anything that felt new and different which was practically *everything,* created panic.

Old *Is* New

Every life situation had become new again. Every place I'd ever been to was something, as a brain injured person, I was experiencing for the first time. Every person I'd ever known regardless of how long, be it family, friend or acquaintance became a new connection. Even if I was in one of those periods where I thought and felt like I knew everyone, as long as they were in their proper place, including people on the bus, then every encounter was fresh and new; except when it wasn't then it was just plain scary and to be avoided.

I never knew what to expect in any situation because I no longer had the power of anticipation. This deficit of not having prior warning, expectation or knowledge of what was to come, in any situation, would prove to be extremely challenging for me and those with whom I was to become involved with romantically or otherwise.

CHAPTER VI- Sick & Twisted Relationships

March 2004-January 2005

"...everyone we meet will either be our crucifier or our saviour depending on what we choose to be to them...every relationship takes us deeper into Heaven or deeper into Hell; Marianne Williamson, from A Return to Love.

Some well-meaning friends knew I was in a bind when I was due to go on a cruise, but my cabin-mate, Mary, was no longer in the picture. They introduced me to one of their friends, Stella, and deemed her to be a good substitution for the cruise vacancy. This was great news to me, because the fare had already been paid, and I couldn't face the idea of going on the cruise alone.

Some other dear friends had helped me out with organising and funding, so that I could enjoy a little, much needed vacation which all sounded good, as long as I didn't focus on all the accompanying fear around it.

Stella was to be my new travel mate for the upcoming cruise. I met with her briefly, and asked what I thought were the most important and pertinent questions of someone that I was to spend a week in close quarters with. She passed the exam easily, even though there were some troubling indications which cropped up during the question period, but I'd ignored the red flags because I was just too afraid of the alternative; to go by myself.

It was the end of March, 2004 just a few weeks shy of the 2 year anniversary of my accident. I'd thought to myself then that I should be further along in the healing process. I had expected to be back to work by now; back to my former life.

I had managed, though, to lose a bit of weight from my short, but intense foray back to the gym. I was walking further and longer distances, so I did feel better and in so doing was able to reconnect with more of my body parts. My legs and arms were no longer foreign attributes, dangling out in front somewhere, in my awareness I had reclaimed them.

More Sleep & Sound Problems

Fears and vulnerabilities still plagued my days, and now my nights as my sleeping patterns changed too. Pre-accident, I slept beautifully every night without exception. Now, however, I could not fall asleep. I felt extremely tired and each night I mentally recommitted to a good night's sleep, but none would come. Once I'd managed to get to sleep, usually sometime around 2-4 a.m., I was easily awakened by transient sounds, no matter how soft.

Post-Trauma...

Post–accident sirens always startled me to the point where I would curl-up into a ball, arms wrapped around my knees frozen until long after they passed. This category of sounds was extremely terrifying, and it took many years of desensitisation to get over them.

The building I lived in then was situated on a busy intersection controlled only on 2 sides with stop signs. Often cars stopped at the stop signs, waiting for a break in traffic, would race across the street sometimes cutting off the right-of-way traffic, which was always good for much horn honking and excitement in general. At this same spot was an uncontrolled (without an overhead light) pedestrian cross-walk that was often occupied; an accident magnet. One night I was lying in bed, awake as usual, when I heard the familiar sounds of screeching tires followed by the sound of impact, of metal on something else. My body reacted as it always did, but then something different happened. I came out of the usual self-embrace sooner than ever before.

I don't remember why that happened then, but I'm grateful because I was able to get up and look outside towards the crosswalk to see a car, stopped just in front of the crosswalk, and a person lying on the ground a few feet away. I panicked and pulled back in horror from the window, then ran from one end of my apartment to the other and back several times more.

Eventually I did pick up the phone and call 911, trying to explain to the operator the event and subsequent carnage (in hind sight my behaviour would have seemed somewhat comical). I could not get out the words I wanted to as my brain simply 'flooded', but fortunately after much babbling, it was determined that another concerned person had already reported the accident. What a relief!

I hung up feeling totally rung out and exhausted and thought about what to do next. It took me a while, but eventually, I'd decided to bring a blanket to the fallen person. Scared and feeling sick to my stomach I went outside to confront my demons, or so it felt to me at the time. When I got to the woman lying on the ground, I covered her shaking and unconscious body with the blanket. I didn't even stop to ask any questions, but I just went to her directly. To engage anyone in conversation would have been too much to ask of myself, so I instead acted out of instinct.

Soon the scene looked like a typical accident recovery situation; emergency vehicles and personal running around doing their jobs. I retrieved my blanket from one of them and retreated to my apartment soon after. I was shaken and shaking.

More About Sleep Issues...

Sleep and brain injury are not compatible, at least that was my experience for a very long time, however, your experience may be different.

My earliest understanding of the sleep problem was that a disruption to my brain's Circadian Rhythm had occurred. This inferred that my brain & body would not automatically fall into this rhythm, which controlled when one became sleepy and subsequently woke up. This natural phenomenon is linked to the setting and rising sun and it would initiate a sensation of sleepiness once the sun began to set and darkness fell, then like clock-work, one would gradually awaken with the brightness of a new day. But this was not the case for me.

My sleep rhythm like some other rhythms such as dancing was completely out of whack. My doctor changed around my daily intake of medications, which always helped a little, but nothing significant ever came of this approach. Listening to soothing music or sound was out of question as my brain still couldn't tolerate the variety of sounds typical to music.

For the first time ever, having extremely poor sleep quality was my reality and so too it's cousin, extremely poor quality of waking time.

Back To The Cruise…

Everything was set in stone. I *was* going on a cruise, albeit hesitantly and unfortunately things started and ended badly.

Stella snored horrifically, and even though I'd purchased ear plugs on route at cruise ship prices, I could not hope to sleep through the reverberating sounds she emitted. Nothing, not even kicking her bed helped to abate the assault on my senses, the snorting and snuffling would persist throughout the entire night without interruption.

I remained cheerful however, because I soon forgot about the impossible sleeping arrangement, and instead focused on the cruise itself. I was very tired, but maintained my enthusiasm, after all the simple truth was that I could not have been there without a chaperon- such as she was.

The Trouble With Stella…

The third day of the cruise turned out to be our last day onboard. That night Stella suddenly became very ill and was rushed to the infirmary. As Stella lay in there somewhat catatonic, I was directed by the ship's Doctor to go through Stella's luggage to determine what medications, if any, she was ingesting. In obeying the order, to my huge surprise, I'd discovered two large zip-lock bags stuffed with prescription medications, which I brought directly back to the doctor.

After much deliberating the onboard medical team concluded that she, and anyone deemed to be her travelling companion, me, would have to disembark at the next port-of-call. I felt absolutely crushed under the weight of my disappointment, and withdrew into a kind of shock and trance-like state.

The following morning we were escorted to the nearest hospital in a non-English speaking country, where everyone was much taller, much more intense and it seemed to me that, in general, they did not want us there. The reality was that I didn't want to be there under those circumstances, period.

Once in the hospital people crowded around me, as Stella was wheeled away to the CAT scan room, they demanded cash money and/or my signature of assurance regarding payment for services. I was under the mistaken belief that the insurance company had previously confirmed all the necessary details including authorizing Stella's anticipated medical expenses. After many hours of what felt like an intense interrogation session did the hospital staff come to the realization that one of their own had made the error, then and only then, after much back peddling and apologies was I permitted to leave the hospital, 12 or so hours later.

Meanwhile a stranger, fellow tourist who watched the entire drama as it unfolded, kindly gave me a long distance telephone card so I could try to work things out with the insurance company.

In my opinion, travel ordeals are as much a part of travelling as the food, the customs, the sights etc. and if you've ever travelled you know this to be a certainty. While some challenges might get a normally calm person agitated by their inevitable inconveniences, they are quickly forgotten once travel resumes and momentum is restored. That's true for most 'normal' people but I was no longer one of *those* people.

I've had tremendous good fortune and circumstance throughout my life that has afforded me the luxury and privilege of travel along with the thrills that travel adventure brings. Many times during my wanderings, I was forced to recalculate, rework or in rare cases totally abandon my meticulously prepared plans. This could be also viewed as 'just life' but it is even more so when referring to travel.

So it's with that discourse in mind that I embarked on the cruise, and maintained my optimism, at least until things started to go sideways.

Throughout the Stella ordeal, I struggled to maintain my equilibrium on a moment to moment basis, never quite achieving the goal, which was to get back to my center. I vacillated between the extremes of looking and feeling panic-stricken or shut-down; looking fearful or withdrawn or both until eventually just defaulting to *disconnected* in order to just cope.

Slowly the reality sunk in to the point where I realised that I needed to find a place to crash for a night or two. Stressed out and exhausted, I scoured the phone book, which fortunately had a few English ads for hostels, made a few calls then cabbed to the one with the most pleasant sounding name; Tranquillity Bay, I could really go for some of that, I'd thought at the time.

Once checked-in, I dog-napped the proprietor's lab-cross, collapsed on the narrow, well-used mattress and cuddled up with 'Bella', fleas, ticks and all. I couldn't sleep through the brain chatter, so I looked out the window to check-out my view of the bay just in time to see my cruise ship sailing away. That did it. I'd break down shortly thereafter.

Three days later, and after plenty more drama, I got on a plane with Stella in tow and we headed home, back to Vancouver.

That experience became a major turning point for me

emotionally, and mentally. I took tremendous confidence from the fact that I handled, as well as I could, every difficult and stressful moment that was thrown in my direction. I didn't dwell on the 'facts' i.e. choosing the wrong travel mate, wasn't stable enough to travel etc., simply because in doing so I would have missed the most valuable take-away; yes those things were true, and yes they did reinforce my feeling vulnerable, but, I-got-through-it! And that's what stuck in my brain.

One really neat, cosmic experience that happened while all of that was going down was that I got the opportunity to repay the kind soul who gave me the LD Phone card. On route to a bird sanctuary, on a very isolated off-the-beaten-path road, my cabbie and I came across 2 people stranded out in the 40C+ heat. I insisted we stop and pick them up and take them to wherever they were headed. Not remembering faces or names was and continues to be a huge challenge for me and that day was no exception. The dutiful driver loaded the two thirsty travellers then crammed their copiously packed bags into every available space inside the small compact.

The couple were so thankful to be rescued from the mid-day tropical sun and I was just happy to help. Within minutes, one of them, a young girl, said, "Hey, I know you!" That's impossible?! I thought, and so became stuck on that thought until she added, "I saw you at the hospital a few days ago, and how is your friend? How are you?!"

"Huh? Oh my God! It's you! You gave me the phone card!"

Uproarious laughter and jubilation ensued.

Wow, how cool is that?!

The chapter heading is 'sick and twisted relationships' which refers to my choices in the people I attracted during my recovery from BI.

Stella was someone that I wouldn't have normally associated with simply because we didn't hang out in the same social circles. She was funny and intelligent and was also a mirror for my fears and mistrust of people, places and things.

This type of attraction whether for friendship or otherwise, to someone filled with fears and who consequently isolated themselves from the world, was to become yet another recurrent theme in my BI recovery; in other words people just like (the new) me.

Once home, the remnants of the cruise played out as never-ending drama spanning weeks and months, and the strained relationship with Stella deteriorated into a full-on battle of wills. Mercifully, we stopped communication altogether which facilitated some healing, but that was not to last before the next big issue surfaced. It was suspected that I had contracted a parasite while abroad.

I lost some weight, which never happens on a cruise, and felt really awful. The accompanying blows to my spirit and self-esteem were devastating, especially since my health was already pretty unstable and declined further still, even after the proper medications could be prescribed.

Michelle As A Stalker

Within a month of all this happening, I would soon become attracted to someone who worked at the deli counter in a funky grocery store that I often frequented (to buy all those cookies!) when going to my various medical appointments.

She was kind, funny and articulate but fear-filled and shy too; my type- exactly!

I would often go there for no other reason than to catch a glimpse of her as she labored behind the counter graciously and dutifully fulfilling all the demands of the upscale crowd that the store catered to. I'm sure it took weeks before I had the courage to speak to her, then several weeks more until I eventually gave her my number.

In hindsight, I must have freaked her out with my nervous behaviour and yet she seemed to enjoy the conversations we had and intimated to me that she wanted to try a yoga class sometime. I took her comment as an invitation for more contact. I then ramped things up to the next level; an invitation to try a yoga class with me.

Even now, this episode of my past is so hard to talk about and to admit to; I was deeply disturbed by my behaviour then, as I am now but for different reasons.

Back when it was happening, I felt scared thus battled the constant, overriding fear that no one would ever want to be with me in such a damaged state and this desperation led me to places, in thought and behaviour, which I would not normally have ventured.

And now, I just feel sadness for that person who *was* me, and knowing too, that many others fall into the same kind of desperation post trauma, and that they no longer act in alignment with their value systems.

'Sandy', to me, was another lost soul of sorts which is why I was able to latch onto to her so quickly. She wore glasses that were held together with a gnarled and dirty piece of duct tape, naturally, that made her even more attractive to me as it signified struggle and lack which were also persistent themes in my *new* and *old* life.

This was our mutual meeting place, our own private, petit café, where we connected in spirit.

Soon after though her smiles became looks of dread but I didn't take the hints because I couldn't pick up on them. I knew something was off, but couldn't quite grasp what it all meant. The bigger picture eluded my comprehension, and I'd become trapped in a small, in-the-moment, view of the world but this wasn't a 'Zen Moment', rather a distorted and distracted version of the *present one*.

My brain behaved like corrupted computer programming; viruses running amok creating glitches and errors with the output data. I didn't trust my own thought processes, I knew something wasn't jiving with reality, but how to fix it? How to guard against the constant awareness of these lurking Trojans; knowing that my thinking was somehow inherently flawed?

At some point in this process, I became obsessed and continued to go back to the deli long after the invitation had been, quite obviously, rescinded. Sandy's behaviour mirrored my own; desperate and edgy or just plain creepy and eventually I got the message. Her fear of me finally penetrated the brick wall that was my comprehension and things suddenly became painfully obvious that my presence both seriously disturbed her being, and disrupted her life.

The realisation made me feel sick on the inside and, I'd imagined, like a freak on the outside.

I had involved some dear friends in my delusion as well. They, at my insistence came into the deli to scout out my new 'love-interest' and would periodically ask about 'us' which invariably led to me feeling caught in never-ending cycles of self-loathing and self-disgust but worst of all; complete self-rejection.

Years passed before I developed enough courage, and sanity, to go back to the deli (on more than a few occasions) to make amends for my behaviour to Sandy, unfortunately though, she was gone and I never saw her again.

Lack of Understanding *of* Lack of Impulse Control!

I had heard the words uttered by myself and others in what were by now my *previous life* and my *former friends*, always directed towards those we deemed to be the troubled souls, the people with *obvious issues*.

I thought, then, that I'd had a perfect grasp of its meaning especially since there were countless persons around me whom I believed qualified as candidates for this cliché. This included anyone who fell outside the *norms* according to my narrow views about people in general. Such as anyone overweight, unkempt, those engaged in disease-promoting habits, not disciplined (not *like* me), bored with life (also not *like* me), depressed and just generally downtrodden etc., etc. In other words, people coping with life struggles expressed by their obvious externalized physical side-effects and ineffectual coping behaviours, were the people that simply lacked Impulse Control, in my imperfect opinion.

What *I really* lacked, besides compassion and empathy, was insight into the issue of impulse control-this would soon change though, without any contribution from me.

The moment I became brain injured, the alchemic process of turning ignorance into insight, intolerance into acceptance and pity into empathy, had begun.

I realize too, that my opinions and impressions of others then, did not capture the aura of 'Yogi-like', however, at the time the mind of the 'popular culture' that I was allied with, blamed the person for their life's predicaments. This explains too why I was so hyper-critical of myself and others; "your life was your responsibility so clean it up *and* stop complaining about it", was my oft quoted mantra.

As is sometimes said in AA meetings, quitting drinking then cleaning up the mess that our former life created, is simple, not easy, but doable!

I *had* already cleaned it up-of alcohol, drug and tobacco dependencies; switched to a vegetarian diet, and then fought the good fight for the animals (still do!), banished old, self-limiting beliefs such as uncoordinated, incapable, unworthy, not lovable and undeserving; discovered meditation along with a community who were dedicated to mindfulness, Guru-devotion and scripture study. I became a whole person complete with boundaries, adjusted attitudes, appropriate reactions and supreme confidence - a neat and tidy package.

So it was with this assertiveness of mind that I had absorbed, analyzed and deduced my conclusions about everything and everyone. It took a tsunami of adversity to create a ripple of upheaval in my world. There were troubles brewing on the job front and maybe some big changes too, but I had a knack for not dwelling on things which I deemed out of my control.

My relationship to Mary was probably going to run its *short* course, the temporary health issues were *temporary*, and my employment strife too would have eventually petered out. No-thing lasts forever, that was another of my mantras, thus I worried little about what I'd come to understand as the Maya (illusion & drama) of the material world.

My view of myself as a student of Yoga and Eastern Philosophy scripture was that of 'Yogi in-training' which was an idea promoted and nurtured by the spiritual community I belonged to plus, I'd enjoyed a Bliss-Factor of 10 to prove it!

To get through the experience of being brain injured, I would often remark that it required me to draw upon everything I'd ever done and learned (up to the point of impact). Such as all the self-improvement stuff I did to get well and move beyond the limiting and destructive belief models from my childhood, but even that work as tremendous as it was, did not give me a frame of reference, or the context, for the challenges I faced, as a brain injured person.

But Back To *My* Lack Of Impulse Control...

Trying to hang on to money and track spending became more like a mystery to be solved than a budget matter, although to even suggest I followed a budget then would be a colossal stretch of the imagination. I just went through money without any mental or physical connection to the act of spending.

Where did all the money go? Good question!

I had an injury which, by its very origin (the brain!), created a perfect storm of runaway, unaccountable and un-trackable behaviours. Unless someone was willing to shadow my every move and act as my memory and critical thinker, there would be no record of the mounting financial transactions. I knew I frequented the ATM machines as evidenced by the volume of receipts stashed away in my wallet, but I didn't *recall actually withdrawing the money.* This strange phenomenon was, as I mentioned before, a passing mystery; one that would fade away as quickly as it arose in my mind. It would take years and a Personal

Bankruptcy to reconstruct a portion of the emotional carnage and financial havoc, this chaotic behaviour wreaked in my life.

Only after developing sufficient discipline and desire and most critically, self-compassion and forgiveness, did I begin to change the ruinous outcomes of this pattern of spending.

I wouldn't say that I now have a complete handle on spending, but having a legitimate, workable budget has made me more accountable and feeling less tortured hence, less stressed, about money than ever before.

Lack of impulse control showed-up in other areas too, like the non-stop talking *and* its cousin, non-stop interrupting of others *trying* to speak! The latter problem was more disconcerting to me because I had always considered myself to be an excellent listener; it was something I'd worked at. Listening and being a good listener was important to me, as command of those two habits symbolized respect and consideration, the two things I was especially pleased with within myself and practiced towards others.

If you've ever experienced the frustration and exasperation of trying to communicate with someone who constantly interrupts and speaks over your words then you will have suffered *me* and my annoying habits, in some other person. I'm truly sorry, because I know it must have been dreadful! The good news is I'm still working on it.

Other examples of impulse control typical of some brain injured persons that I've *not* experienced (gratefully), but have heard plenty about from these people, are sexual dysfunction and hyper-sexuality. I think I had enough on my plate, but am truly sympathetic to those who experienced sexual impulses that were devastating to their lives and the lives of others.

Sexual dysfunction manifested in my life too, but not as impulsiveness or uncontrollable urges, but in the way that I now lacked the ability to anticipate my partner's needs.

This was a crushing blow to my already dis-abled sense of self-worth.

Katrina, A Face From My Past...

'Katrina' reappeared in my life after a very brief period of self-consoling from the painful loss of my purely psychological romantic-partnership with Sandy, the Deli-Girl.

She, Katrina, had run across a good friend of mine when the subject of me came up. Numbers were exchanged, and when I got an enthusiastic phone call from my friend, Anita, I was still feeling sad but curiously too, ready to move on. I might have been a little suspicious of my willingness to jump right in to the next thing, but the overriding state of feeling rejected trumped all other emotional possibilities.

In a short period of time, Katrina and I were not only hanging out but considered a couple (of crazy people I'd later suggest!).

Within 3 weeks of publicly declaring our new 'girlfriend' status there was trouble. Katrina's anger issues bubbled up much sooner than my abilities to manage them, and at six weeks I was journaling that I felt like how a battered woman, I imagined, must feel.

I was so far out of my comfort zone with this person, that soon all my shaky boundaries of self-preservation were not only crossed but effectively obliterated. I'd lost the ability to defend myself without the capacity to commit to their purpose-that was to have a sense of safety in all situations. The next several months were ones of deep emotional struggles, and adding to them was the crazy fact that I'd donated all my winter clothing; hats, gloves, toques, footwear and parkas to the local ministry responsible for establishing new Canadian residents who had come to Canada from Africa. It had seemed like a really great idea at the time, in the middle of summer and 30C!

My friends later confessed to me that they had planned an intervention of sorts, but that their shock and disbelief in my choice of partner kept them, for a time at least paralyzed with doubt regarding what to do about it exactly.

My sexual performance insecurities grew with every

attempt at intimacy and soon I felt utter dread at the prospect of it. I no longer sensed my partner's needs or desires and my own ability for enjoyment was seriously dampened. My lack of sensory sensitivity was due in part to me taking necessary prescription medications to deal with the constant and uninterrupted, terrible, physical pain.

The primary culprit though, was that I consistently felt like I was just no good at anything anymore so the experience of being inept, particularly in matters of sexual performance, was emotionally crippling.

My new-life experience as brain injured became a sequence of failures which served to cement in my psyche the overriding internal suspicion, that I was simply a total mess of a person.

I journaled daily throughout this Katrina period and through the process of writing and more writing, I discovered that I was indeed behaving like a battered woman. The reality was so gut-wrenching to me and I'd ask myself, out loud and to no one in particular, how did this happen?! How did I get to this place?!

Very soon though, something new and unfamiliar would start to assert itself into my awareness, something I'd sensed at first as an upset stomach coupled with chest tightness. I realized what I felt was dread.

Katrina and I broke-up soon after Christmas and just before Valentine's Day. Soon after it began, it was done, and I was both relieved and afraid; something else much worse than rejection was lurking in the background, behind all the usual chattering of my mind, and I'd felt deathly afraid of it. So much so that at the time, to stay in a toxic relationship seemed a better alternative to being on my own but *now,* I was alone.

Rediscovering Music, Kind Of...

During my time with Katrina there were two other significant self-discoveries that brought my life a measure of joy. For the first time since the accident I was able to listen to music, sort of. This music came in the form of live spoken-word performances accompanied by a single beat of sound accompanied by the artist's own sound-effects. It was a huge breakthrough for me and I was extremely ecstatic about the prospect of listening to even more complex sounds.

Since I wasn't yet able to drive more than an hour without becoming completely exhausted, I resorted to begging my friends to take me to Seattle, a four-hour return trip, to see these amazing animated poets in action. Once at the venue I'd scout out the biggest and most comfortable sofa and settle in for the 60-90 minute show. I could rest or nap if necessary, which I often did, drifting off to the soft regular beats of this verbalized version of music.

Eventually, my friends no longer wished to come on these late night trips and it hadn't occurred to me to look for local acts, because I didn't yet think beyond the immediate. I did come across some really great local talent and added a handful of cd's to my new 'music' collection. Katrina's artistic connections and ambitions helped me to further explore the world of poetry and music and for that I'm so grateful.

Also during this time of exploration, I joined a djembe drumming group to try to learn how to stimulate my brain into forming new neural pathways through the playing of musical instruments. Unfortunately, it was about as successful as my brief foray into guitar playing, which was around the same time. Not to say these attempts were total disasters but my self-confidence did take a few hits.

What became crystal clear was that I wasn't sufficiently coordinated in mind or body to pull off either endeavour, so they were both eventually abandoned. (I forgot to mention however, that I was a semi-success at clacking two sticks together!)

What I noticed during these attempts at brain restoration was that I seemed to be missing a mental connection when it came to thinking and doing things simultaneously. I could think out the act but was not able harmonize it with my body. To put it another way, I knew what to do and could mentally speak the command to my body but that's where things fell apart. My body didn't or couldn't follow the commands. It, my body, would freeze or do something completely off in the opposite direction that my mind was trying to steer it in; like a car that veers off to the right whenever you turn the steering wheel left. How does a person fix that? I didn't know how.

All that was soon forgotten, including the growing suspicion that I was somehow terribly flawed, so I was off to next new thing before the feelings became too big to manage.

If It's Not Written Down It Doesn't Exist!

At the same time when I was challenging myself to play a musical instrument and making attempts at being more sociable, I was also trying to reincorporate list-making back into my routine. Pre-injury, I always utilized lists to the point where, my home, my car, even my workspace was plastered with them and I believed too that I knew their every spot and their every purpose.

With that in mind, I couldn't figure out why I hadn't thought of list-making sooner. Of course I would have to remember to write the list first before reaping all its benefits. Simple, but not easy!

"You Don't Need Me To Write It Down, YOU Just Need To Remember!"

Around this time I'd realized that some family and friends were becoming increasingly frustrated with what they perceived as my lack of will power and/or just plain laziness. My inability to remember became, in some situations, a personal affront to them and their serenity. To be fair, I was challenging to be around. In most situations, I didn't remember most of the details like who, what, where or when, coupled with the fact that many of these same people were still struggling to locate Michelle under all the chaos that was now me.

I would very soon understand into my journey of recovery

that most of the people I had surrounded myself with, pre-accident, needed me to perform at the top of my game or there could be some unpleasant consequences. I positioned myself as the go-to person both personally and professionally; I needed to be needed and was extremely reliable, but was becoming less so even before the brain injury.

I think the pre-injury pressure, to be everything to everyone, carried itself over into my new life because, prior to my injury, this pressure had already begun to create more than a few cracks in the veneer that was my near-perfect life.

...but back to the list making...

I'd begun ever so slowly to re-introduce this memory-nudging technology back into my life. But *to remember,* that was the one thing that hijacked my every attempt at getting past a problem; many of my problems began, progressed and ended with the challenge of poor memory, short-term memory to be precise.

If I remembered to write the list, the next roadblock was then actually taking it out of my pocket to look at it. That's a three or four step process which is probably one or two steps too many for someone in my brain-injured state!

It's hard to imagine that something this simple took so long to incorporate into my routine, such as it was, but it did. One big contributing factor, I think was the overriding self-limiting belief, that if I just tried harder, and really applied myself, I *would* remember without a list or any other kind of memory enhancing technique.

Ultimately though, after years of not being able to prove this theory, I would eventually embrace list-making once again, and begin to reap its many benefits.

And today nearly eleven years later, I rely on post-it type notes, as an extension of my memory, when I remember to look at them that is! My home and my car continue to be plastered in sticky-notes, plus they seem to turn up in the dryer most laundry days.

Also too, several electronic devices fill in the gaps nicely. Their only drawback, however, is when the reminder chime goes off, I still forget *what for* and *why now,* until I physically look at the device emitting the chime.

What can I say except that I continue to be a work-in-progress!

"Dying Is Easy. Living Is The Challenge!"

Between toxic relationships, trying to play the guitar & drum, and some failed attempts at getting organised, I could see how living as the new-me could be more than I'd bargained for (and I hadn't recalled bargaining for anything remotely close to this life!).

I didn't yet consider opting out of my life, but had the bitter-sweet realization that dying would have been easier, albeit much less interesting, I presumed. The challenges of living this new life would just keep coming until the grief became unbearable and, for a short time, I seriously considered other options.

CHAPTER VII- THE BEGINNING OF GRIEF

February -August 2005

*"Our deepest grief is reserved for things that have no acceptable substitutes; loved ones, relationships, heath, hopes, dreams...*from: Finding your own North Star, by Martha Beck

That *thing lurking* that I become aware of feeling, but had been unconsciously resisting, at last spilled out into my daily living as moods of anguish, coalesced with uncontrollable sobbing and I felt different inside; this was *new*, it was grief.

Outwardly the grief spread to nearly every corner that was my life. The insurance claim really started to heat up with copious amounts of lawyer correspondence, face to face interrogations with Insurance Company lawyers (erroneously called Examinations for Discovery) and an impending personal financial bankruptcy.

Inwardly, I felt as contorted as all the external dramas; my health, still suffering from the presumed parasitic invasion that I'd contracted while on the 'cruise' and the overwhelming grief generated by the recent relationship break-up; all conspiring to topple my existence, a kind of house of cards that was already in a very fragile state of being.

Adding to this chaos was that my previous decision to move was now suddenly coming into fruition. I no longer had any protective barriers with which to cope with the onslaught of stress. The grief that had been so patient in the past now seemed poised to explode with a vengeance. Eventually what happened was not so much an explosion but rather a slow and steady primordial ooze of unacknowledged fears.

My next move began amid this turmoil...

Soon one of my siblings and I would have a terrible falling out over money and several previous unresolved resentments. In the past, I could manage these differences of opinion with more grace, but that was all gone now and instead felt deeply hurt and abandoned by my family. In reality though, we were a fractured and dysfunctional tribe right from our earliest beginnings, and the current rift was just one more attempt at trying to behave like a *real, normal* family.

Packing up my things was a little easier this time, as I had somehow managed to become more organised by utilizing my recently rediscovered list-making skills. I was extremely tormented though, at the prospect of leaving my little heritage apartment. Much change in me had happened while I lived there, and I felt hyper-sensitive and hyper-emotional about leaving my little town as well. Dealing with any new thing now felt like an impossible situation with no way around or through, just the experience of anguish.

I now noticed how easily I cried which was also new. I remember sitting at the window waiting for the movers to come and feeling completely conflicted about the move, and I nearly called them to cancel at the last possible minute but just couldn't seem to act or follow through. I continued to sit there in excruciating emotional pain, wrestling with my thoughts up to and until the moment the movers arrived.

Once fully loaded, the moving van pulled up next to my new place, a small former gardener's cottage situated off a busy back-alley in downtown Vancouver, I'd been at a complete loss as to how to decide where my things were to go. I'd defaulted to instructing the movers to put most of everything except for the obvious bed, sofa and bookshelf, into the tiny little garage attached to the cottage.

Once moved, the long and painful job of unpacking commenced, dragging on for months, as I frequently needed to take days off, away from any boxes and the subsequent decisions they would inevitably bring.

Another side-effect of coming into grief was the emergence

of anger. This was different from the frustration I was regularly experiencing this, was *real* ire, not brought on by some specific event or minor irritation, but rather it bubbled up alongside the grief. Perhaps they were just two sides of the same emotion, but either way, my world was never going to be the same, after the arrival of these two uninvited cohorts.

Once my kitchen was sorted out somewhat, I had started to take better care of myself nutritionally, taking some tentative and difficult steps towards the reclamation of my health. I abandoned all sweets, dairy and meat, while opting for the prolonged cleansing diet of strictly raw foods. I let go of green tea and went through the short, but intense period of caffeine withdrawal. I learned to sprout food from seeds and make fresh nut milks made of almonds, walnuts and hazelnuts. I also drank my own freshly pressed wheatgrass and other fruit and veggie juice concoctions every morning.

My new food regime while labour intensive, was a good distraction from all the other stuff which, in my mind, conspired to keep me stuck. Plus taking better care of myself helped me to believe that I could get better; a lot better in fact.

Re-Learning To Speak In Complete Sentences

I started to read books again in an attempt to reclaim the English language. The BI had severely handicapped my ability to not only retrieve words, but comprehend them as well. I had also forgotten how to spell and use grammar in a proper sentence.

I didn't suffer from the more complex and debilitating condition of *aphasia,* another side-effect of brain injury, but did struggle to participate in conversations both verbal and digital such as email. Spell checks are great, except I knew I wouldn't relearn the basics of English vocabulary if I didn't take more risks. I needed to try to get out of my comfort zone of safe people, and some situations, like being alone, for example.

The loss of comprehension of grammar surfaced in my

previous relationship and was a painful and shame-filled reminder of the now obvious damage to my *social self.* Yet another loss, but I didn't yet have the emotional or mental strength to analyze it too closely. Instead, I got busy with other matters which generated feelings of gratification and hope. These were the things I thought I could control.

The phenomenon of thought *flooding* can occur most commonly for those with BI and can be extremely embarrassing. It's the point in any conversation where the BI person suddenly and inexplicably is unable to continue to speak any thoughts. This could manifest itself on a person's face as a look of being completely stunned or afraid or both. Sometimes too, I would feel so perplexed in the moment, forgetting the subject or origin of the conversation, I would forget who I'd just been talking to or what the conversation was even about. Outwardly and inwardly I'd look and feel stuck.

I guess one could say that my state of self, at that moment, was at the very least synchronized, and that was *something* to hang onto.

Trying New Things And Meeting New People

My new neighborhood was fitting of that designation; it was authentic, busy and cultural, it was a *real* neighborhood.

My new daily habits included the short walk to the co-op grocer, and then a visit to the local organic veggie stand, housing a tiny raw food café that soon became my new hangout.

There I met like-minded raw foodies and other health focused types with whom I could chat with, using short well-constructed sentences.

Over time, this gave me the confidence to take even greater conversational risks like vocalizing longer more refined thoughts into comprehensive opinions. Mostly, I kept to the short and manageable concepts, as I continued to be perplexed by the notion of the 'social cues' when conversing and had a hard time knowing when to interject and when to listen or, the most elusive cue; when to end a conversation.

The worst moment would come when invariably, I wouldn't pick up on the many subtle hints indicating that the conversation had run its natural course, and was now over. That moment was always very embarrassing and very awkward.

Perhaps most of these people thought of me as just a little slow, maybe even more than a little. Whatever their true feelings, I always felt welcomed and celebrated as the person I was by their genuine warmth and kindness. These people by way of their gentle, unconditional acceptance, made it so much easier for me take the risks.

Connecting With Former Friends And New Acquaintances

Re-learning the skills of conversations allowed me to take the unprecedented step towards forming new friendships, and rebuilding some former connections.

I met quite a few people through the raw food scene, and while I learned a lot from many of them, I generally didn't participate so much, as just listen to their philosophies on food. It's so true that mostly everyone has an opinion on pretty much everything. So it was a fortuitous convergence of my inability to communicate effectively, and the need of others to talk incessantly about what they knew and believed to be the gospel regarding a Raw Food diet.

I also reconnected with a TRG person, Debbie. We began with long phone conversations that led to exploring some of the local music & poetry scene. I suddenly began to feel very self-conscious about my physical appearance. I was too thin and looked, in general, absolutely wretched!

This was all happening during the late winter to early summer, 2005, and so for another very brief period of time, life seemed to take on new hope for me.

Hope rapidly faded, however, as despite all my efforts to recapture health and well-being, I only managed to stay ever so slightly ahead of, that by now, had become a vast fountainhead of grief.

Descent Into The Void That Is Grief

By July, the wheels of my recovery had become completely detached- spinning off in every direction. I had continued to drop weight to the point where I only weighed 89 lbs, an incredible thirty-three pounds underweight! Something would have to give then, and while I pondered the idea of going back to cooked foods, my beloved cat, Martin, who was seven years old then, bit me on the hand while I was attempting to pick him up.

I was in a hurry to get to an appointment because, as was the norm then, I was usually running late. I quietly, a little too quietly came up on him from behind which resulted in him being terribly spooked. He reacted to the fright with a quick reflexive bite, sinking his long, sharp incisors deep into the large knuckle of one of my fingers.

The pain was immediate and searing, but I don't even remember as much as an "ouch", which is bizarre because shrieking would have been perfectly appropriate at the time!

I did manage to get Martin back into the house however, but in the fracas, the impending appointment was totally forgotten.

About hour or so later, one of my siblings arrived with her teenage daughter. They were on their way to snowboard camp in Whistler, and had planned to crash on my sofa-bed for the night. I had completely forgotten that they were coming, and felt absolutely devastated by the cat bite, so simply shut down in order to cope with all the demands on my attention.

I visited with my relatives, ignoring the swelling mass that was my hand. By the evening, I noticed the redness in my hand had spread to the top of my shoulder. However, I was feeling unable to react to it, and I simply went to bed trying, unsuccessfully, to sleep through the horrible pain.

The next morning, we all went shopping as my niece

seemed convinced that she was in dire need of new clothes. My recollection of that day is quite vague, except for the periodic hallucinations. Only once my family had left, around 5 pm, did I entertain the possibility of going to the hospital.

I drove around Vancouver in a fog, not able to think through the situation until eventually I arrived, some hours later, at the emergency ward of St Paul's Hospital. Once there, before I received any treatment and quite appropriately so, I first received plenty of condemnation and disapproving comments regarding taking my sweet time to get there!

Over the next two weeks, I had gone through ten solid days of IV antibiotic therapy, minor hand surgery and many pain killers. Also, hand physiotherapy was to commence shortly.

This all happened around my 43rd birthday.

Some dear friends thought it would be a great idea to surprise me with a personal visit, holding a burning candle-topped cake in hand.

My sister had returned after dropping off her daughter, and joined me for another night before heading home. Her visit came just in time to see me in a terrible state, with my hand bandaged nearly up to the elbow and me looking very unwell, emotional fragile and much too thin.

Just before she was to head out the door, my intrepid friends arrived with their little surprise. Their timing was so bad and so perfect all at the same time. I had been barely hanging on until the moment my sister departed, so that I could then collapse on my bed. Instead, I would have to suffer a little longer.

As they came into my little house gleefully singing the happy birthday song, while emanating beautiful expressions of joy and love, I burst into tears.

The moment became one of awkward consoling, and eventually I was able to collect my fragile-self enough to, and with an apologetic tone, thank them then have a piece of cake.

The perfection of their visit came when I later realised, that my friends and family had never seen me in such a compromised state, which must have been a hard, but necessary shock to their systems.

I was the 'rock' in my circle. That's not to say that they didn't have strengths, they did, but I never fell apart or had a crisis, not ever.

I had periods in my past of difficulty like situational depression, when I was 24 years old. During that time I had left my husband then went from living in a nice home to a shabby basement suite with no windows. Shortly after that I moved to another, much larger city. Eventually I crashed hard and my usual enthusiasm for life quickly got used up. My drink & drug habits first multiplied, and then cubed themselves in severity and frequency.

I would soon find myself on the Greyhound heading for Vancouver, where I had received good help, and my employer approved a permanent transfer.

I left my family and all my friends behind. My entire support system dissolved.

Eventually I learned to live differently, and realised too that sometimes you have to run away to get well, I know I did.

But Back To The Grief....

I sat in my little cottage after everyone had left, at last, and did what I been trying to do all day, break down and let myself be the mess that I was.

If the *mess* that was, self-serving lawyers, insurance company nastiness, illness, pain, confusion, self-deflation, self-pity and still more pain had been confined to that day, okay then I probably would not have sunk to even lower levels, but it had to run its course, so I would hold on for the inevitable ride to the bottom.

Days morphed into weeks of crying and wailing, until the inevitable conclusion was reached, out of desperation and despair. During this bleak period, I vacillated between the two extremes of suicidal and homicidal, but gratefully, never quite settling on either one.

Eventually I did get some more good help, and this time the counsellor used a technique called EMDR, Eye Movement Desensitisation and Reprocessing, which proved to be huge. This provided more emotional and mental breakthroughs for me.

Within a few short months of treatment and supportive counselling I was better, a lot better, and subsequently, I was able to crawl out of the dungeon that was despair and move forward, only this time with purpose.

CHAPTER VIII-ADDING UP THE LOSES

August 2005-March 2006

"Acceptance of a loss does not signify that the pain has gone away. It only refers to a level of pain that is tolerable and has become mild enough to become part of your comfort level"...from Objects in the Mirror are Closer than they Appear

The presence of anger was an indication to me of the emergence of an emotional healing cycle. At one point, the anger had reached raging proportions around my perceived and actual injustices, perpetrated on me by the legal system.

The details aren't as important as the residue of these experiences, which for me was the birth of acceptance.

Confronting The Losses...
A shift in my perspective had begun. My counselling continued for many more months, and perhaps if I'd gotten there sooner, I wouldn't have sunk so low. However, I believe we ask for help in our own time, and for some poor souls, not at all.

Everywhere I looked I saw the reality of my life. I noticed things now with much more lucidity. Another fog had lifted, only this time there was clarity not just another bank of more fog.

An insurance company lawyer once remarked to me, "It's Your Funeral!" It took me a while to turn it around to use her comment as a springboard for change, but there it was. I decided that in fact it was a good time for a funeral. It was the perfect time to re-invent myself.

In order to embrace the new Michelle, I had to first understand who she was, but also, who she no longer was.

I quickly got down to business and made a list.

Reliving my history was always difficult then, as this exercise brought up all the grief again, but I now knew I could at least handle some of the loss by putting it in its appropriate category of *before* and *after*. Now, there *was* an after, where I could create anew from the ashes of my former life.

My lists contained all the ideals that I thought defined me along with their corresponding losses as related to their, emotional, mental, spiritual and physical aspects. This took many months to complete, because the stress of it meant I would need to take periodic breaks. I had to absorb and accept (in principle) each loss.

What I came up with in the end was a shocker. For the most part up until then, I had drifted through my days mostly oblivious to my surroundings, which included the totality of the character that *was* I, Michelle.

Who was this 'I'?

Who I was *no longer* became crystal clear. I was not a partner nor a good/best friend, not a teammate, a workmate or a mate of any kind, not the motivator, the counsellor or the fixer, neither the witty conversationalist nor enthusiast. Since the accountability and dependability factors were at an all-time low, by default, I'd also lost the birthright designation of sister, daughter and auntie. When I could no longer show up as these personas, I had forfeited their fundamental privileges too, such as being a good example, mentoring, and my all-time favorite, to have a personal enthusiastic fan-club of nieces and nephews.

All of these things, which *were* my life, vaporized into the ether, in an instant.

It was time to figure out what I wanted. The process felt eerily similar to that of when I was in my late teens. I would spend many hours in the day, obsessing about what to do with my life, but more specific, *who* do I want to be for the rest of my life?

I didn't yet know the answers to the question of who I was, but I decided that despite this, I could *live* differently.

With much trepidation I dragged my bike out of its hiding place, and set my sights on overcoming one traumatic loss at a time. I then dropped the raw diet, and adopted veganism instead. Almost immediately, my body weight at long last began to normalize.

After much sorting and confusion, I managed to get the essential gear assembled for a short, test bike ride. My bike pedals were the clip-less variety, which required I snap into them with special clips. These were permanently affixed to the outer soles of my riding shoes. I thought to myself then, that it was going to be dodgy at first, but my determination was peaking so if I could somehow just seize the moment and get back on the 'horse' I knew I'd be ok, eventually!

Those first few strides were nervous and shaky ones, but within a few blocks, I had settled back into the saddle, and had slowly become aware of the gentle breeze against my face. I then felt the overwhelming and familiar sensation of *freedom*.

This was completely different from my first attempt to get back on my bike. That initial frightening experience came when I had returned to the gym briefly the previous year. I had thought then, (through the fog that was my thoughts) "wouldn't it be a great idea to ride my bike the 5+ kilometers there and back?"

Actually, to be precise I did have one other, prior, attempt at riding my bike. It was very close to the time after the accident, and I hadn't yet fully grasped what had happened to me. I had tried to get back to 'normal' as quickly as possible. I got on my bike and rode for too far and too long. I had been absolutely wasted, in every way it is possible to be wasted. I hadn't been able to give my bike a second look for several years after that. The experience then, felt too humiliating to face.

Looking Outward Instead Of (Just) Inward

The freedom of riding my bike was short-lived but that was okay with me. I'd ridden just long enough to rediscover some of the world around me. In that act of discovering, one of my earliest drives, which was to be outside in the fresh air, I was re-awakened.

During that time, I would take regular trips to a nearby beach on the ocean, which I'd pretty much forgotten even existed. Smelling the salt air, feeling the sand on my bare skin, watching the gulls compete for food with the crows, listening to the waves and all the other enumerable complexities that comprise moving water, for the very first time, again. Life, as it was in these simple life-expressions, was good again.

I continued with counselling, and in doing so begun the laborious work of re-connecting the entities of mind, body and spirit. Slowly, there came the awareness of more pain, but also too, continuity with my thinking body, meaning my thoughts, at times, were emanating from that place inside oneself that is self-identified as the soul or source of intuition.

This period of re-awakening brought unexpected bonuses too. I was suddenly less anxious and much less fearful. This new inner-state came into fruition as a new understanding. This was especially apparent when I was seated across from several, very nasty insurance company lawyers. I had determined that their primary purpose in this life is to de-construct the lives of others, and in doing so, generate sufficient amounts of doubt, that could (and would) successfully undermine the validity of that person's integrity and so too their claim.

That 'person' was me and I suddenly saw that these women, as lawyers, were simply but effectively acting out the roles they had no doubt chosen on some levels of their existence. I dubbed their organisation 'The Bad Actors Guild of BC' or simply 'The BAGS of BC', thus recapturing both my power and sense of humour in one divine moment of fearlessness. I was back, sort of!

Confronting The Pain Of Loneliness

Having the capacity to feel stronger and safer while under pressure was a giant leap forwards however, it did nothing to address the painful feelings of isolation from others.

I did have a few friends who had, for a little while gone away, or had been asked to stay away, but they were back now. I also re-connected somewhat regularly with my friend from TRG, Debbie who, like me, had some cognitive and energy issues. These became our common ground of mutual understanding.

Debbie and I soon hung out more and more, and talked on the phone with consistency. She was going through her own crisis with her current boyfriend, also a trauma survivor, and I allowed myself to be somewhat dragged into the chaos of her life. It gave me some purpose, but also too, unnecessary stress. There was a gradual sliding back into the 'fixer' and 'rescuer' personas; such were my comfort levels with others.

The Perils And Pitfalls Of The 'Legal System', *Not* To Be Confused With A System of Justice!

It was February 2006 and the legal process, I was engaged in, just got a gigantic kick-start.

I made the (big) decision to change my legal representation. I had been talking to a few friends and other lawyers about it, but felt afraid to commit to a major change. It felt a lot like a small child might feel just before they are about to do something they know will bring the wrath down upon them. It created tremendous conflict and chaos within me, but eventually I did take the leap and felt both relieved and guilt-ridden.

I wish I could express how difficult it really was for me then, to go out on a limb and invite even more alienation at a time when I already felt so alone. It was emotional agony, especially since I didn't feel capable of making good decisions. My impulse was to agree with whatever was said as quickly as possible. I didn't yet think things through and I would just react with "Okay!"

I made the change because I felt that the legal process was moving too slowly, and that my well-being was being overlooked. I don't have any regrets about it. My recommendation is however, that if you are in this or a similar predicament, get advice from other lawyers first along with your friends and family. Don't make the decision on your own.

The next few months were filled with countless appointments and counter appointments, to doctors and specialists and still a few others *claiming* to be so.

I was poked, prodded, manipulated, (which was pretty pathetic when you consider my state of being) lied to and harassed. But this was just the normal modus operandi for those 'professionals' who make their living as (well) paid opinion givers for the multitudes of insurance companies.

This was an especially difficult time, and I was still very fragile emotionally. I could be broken down effectively with one or two strategically uttered words. Of all the nasty and unkindness I endured then, nothing was more disappointing and destabilizing than being called a fraud. Unfortunately, I hadn't yet re-grown my covering of thick-skin, thus was highly susceptible to the common legal practice of character-bashing in both oral and written delivery.

Another, New-Beginning

I had been reconnecting with old friends and heard through them about something that really excited me. *That* feeling of excitement, that *felt* different. So, after enduring many months of constant nastiness, trashing and talking, I came to another, life altering decision. I decided it was time to move!

How I pulled this off, I don't really remember, but I did.

I bought a boat!

CHAPTER IX-LIVING VS EXISTING

April & May 2006

"Seek out, or let yourself be guided to, a place where you feel that you can be quiet and clear enough inside to hear or see what you must do to reclaim your life. This can be a special sanctuary or nature spot where you used to go for peace and quiet...from Objects in the Mirror.

Just prior to buying my new home (disguised as a boat), I went on a short trip to visit with my sister. I needed to connect with a friendly face under the backdrop of constant abuses that were endlessly conjured up by the insurance company lawyers and their countless, willing accomplices.

Feeling utterly worn out by the litigation process, I reached out to her in an attempt to mend the prior hurts of unmet expectations of the previous year.

The visit was low-key and succeeded in revitalising our commitment to at least be better at being friends. It was a good start. I returned home in time to prepare for what I anticipated as the inevitable finale to my accident claim.

Moving into a *real* home, something that I could call mine legally meant for the first time in years that I had *some* security. Living in a space of less than 100 square feet meant that I couldn't possibly have any furniture except for a very small TV, plus an equally tiny table with which to set it atop.

At the time, the laborious work required to sort through all my things was much more daunting than I was ever capable of imagining. How had I accumulated so much stuff? It was utterly perplexing and energy zapping, yet, it had to done. I'd called upon a small crew of very dedicated and loyal friends, for their immediate help. Somehow, as is always the way, things got done and in no time I was headed back to the blissful surroundings from where I once lived.

The movers did the all heavy lifting then left me with a huge mountain of 'stuff' that was never going to fit, anywhere nor in any fashion, in the boat. I scrambled but soon found appropriate storage for the nearly 90% of my things, which had to be relocated.

Eventually though everything magically, or so it seemed, came together and at long last I could rest.

Reconnecting With My 'Boat People'

The joy I experienced seeing those beautiful, practically angelic-like faces of my long lost friends was both uplifting and invigorating. Their kindness and generosity was still intact. This *was* home and these people *were* my family.

Some of my closest friends there had been required, by new ministry laws, to relocate their float homes up river to government approved locations.

Luckily for me, they were only a short 5 minute scenic drive along an extensive dyke embankment system, which served as a demarcation point between the river and a fancy new housing development. The drive to their float-home was an extraordinary sight of dilapidated old fishing-industry buildings on one side and cookie-cutter townhomes opposite; both standing in defiance of the other. The bumpy pot-holed lane stretched for many kilometres until you reached my friends new water lot situated a few short strides from an expansive birch tree farm. It was a magical place and I'd visit often.

To say that I simply loved this place would be a tremendous understatement. It represented the peace and bliss that I was still so driven at the time to recapture.

Back at the marina, the office manager determined that my 'slip', the specific dock location of my boat, was appropriate for its size and I would have to wait for another opening if I wanted to relocate it. My boat was situated on an inside 'finger' thus my views were blocked somewhat by several gigantic and elongated, what my friends and I would refer to as, 'Man Boats'. Those were vessels typically owned and driven in nothing less than a maniacal fashion by middle-aged men.

I really wanted a better view of things from my boat, but I would be so wrapped up in the confusion of where to put my things that I didn't have any room or memory to dwell on disappointments, so I stayed where I was and, naturally, this worked out perfectly.

Life was good again. Soon I was actually socializing and having visitors too. I felt connected to myself again in this place of nature and water.

Seeking out the quiet serenity of that community, during what was an extremely intense time in all other aspects of my life, was probably the most important and pivotal decision I'd made so far. Living in close proximity to a support system both in the people, and the natural world stabilized me like nothing else.

Eventually most of my balance difficulties disappeared. There were two opposing camps regarding my decision to live on a boat. My lawyer's position was that I shouldn't take the risk of possibly inviting negative health ramifications so he wasn't happy about it. My family doctor was pleased and suggested that the gentle rocking motion could reset my inner ear, possibly restoring my balance.

I listened to my doctor as he had been there for me for 20 years, through the sudden death of a sibling, my earliest bout with depression, reconstructive nasal surgery, the many lifestyle changes, several relationship endings and beginnings plus the many frequent illnesses and injuries which all paled in comparison to the battle I was presently engaged in.

Even though it was the beginning of April 2006, the weather was still cool and wet and my boat, constructed of aluminum, a material highly conducive to holding the cold (or the heat), made my little cabin space unbearably cold inside.

I would somehow need to remedy that, and do it in a hurry. My two cats were not too impressed either! I forgotten how destabilizing it was for them back when I was renting the boat home (and, as I was constantly reminded then that my rental home was not to be confused with a *proper* boat!). The constant action of the water lapping up against the boat and dock, as well the frequent cyclic movement of the tides & currents could at times be quite disruptive to the serenity and patience of these little creatures. Although the marina was situated on a river, it was only a few short kilometers to the Pacific Ocean and its substantial tidal influences. Adding to their distress were all the other, built-in perils such as, numerous other well-established cats and dogs, the prolific water fowl droppings, which included a few mating pairs of escapee Mute-Swans, and their cygnets (of which the parents could be sometimes aggressively protective of!) Also there were the frequent excessive wakes that created a wave-effect on the dock system from other mobile vessels which also occupied the river waterways but, all these things combined didn't compare to the horrors of, what I referred to as, the dreaded 'poo-slick'.

On several occasions my poor little furred companions actually slipped over-board into one of these flotillas of refuse, expelled from the countless on-board toilets flushed repeatedly throughout the day, each and every day. One could easily observe their terror-filled eyes, as they would frantically paddle, doggy-style, though the piles of floating sewage trying desperately to keep their little heads above it all. Eventually they would spot the dock and climb up one of several old tires that I'd affixed to it specifically for this purpose.

I'd also stashed a pile of old towels nearby just for this type of emergency and after a good bath, followed by many hours of grooming, my little ones would bed down for several days of restoration…until the next time. Gratefully though, this didn't happen very often.

...Back to the challenges of staying warm....

I had some money but in truth, I do not remember where it originated from or how I came to have it. Never the less, it was there so I used some of it, most of it actually, to renovate my little floating palace.

The on-board heating system consisted of an old, very dirty and very stinky diesel-fired stove that I chose not to use and instead relied heavily on electric space heaters, which proved to be terribly inadequate. Soon through my new family of boat-people, I'd been able to get rid of the offensive smelling diesel stove and the accompanying accessories like the fifty gallon diesel-fuel barrel that had been situated externally atop the cabin, also too, all the related pipes and venting tubes. With the massive stove now gone I had a blank canvass with which to impart my new vision. My friend Debbie and I spent a few weeks removing all the old, broken cupboards and shelving so that soon the entire galley was gutted.

In the meantime I cooked using an old camp stove attached to a small propane cylinder which was vented out the nearest window. It was rustic living and reminded me of another one of my favorite, former pastimes, camping.

I realise by now that you must be thinking, "how is it that she appears to manage all these challenges, all of them, with apparent ease?!" Honestly, I was so freaked out at the time by the colossal learning curve I'd taken on that I'd spent many nights curled-up with my cats, crying and wondering, "what in the hell was I thinking?!! "

A few weeks later, I learned enough about the realities of living on a boat to come to the sobering realization that I could not afford to hire anyone to do anything that needed doing. I had just invested, betting all-in, into the proverbial hole-in-the-water-with-which-to-throw-money!

Then, after several more weeks of wondering around absolutely dumb-founded at the reality of my new life, I gathered up my determination and set out to transform my home into the palace that I'd suspected right from the beginning it could be.

I got down to the business of list-making, something I knew I could do, and do well.

It just so happened that some dear boat friends were also cabinet makers. We came to a family-price arrangement for a new set of galley cabinets. The only drawback was that they would take a while to materialize given the nature of the deal. I didn't care though, I was just ecstatic at the prospects of getting some shiny new cupboards.

In the meantime, I really needed to get focused on getting a new fridge as the one I had inherited was a mold factory and it had to go. I tracked down the perfect replacement, a scratch & dent unit created for an apartment dweller. It was ideal. The delivery people brought it as far as the dock next to my boat but no further.

I made the mistake of trying to assist some friends to get it into the boat through a sliding door situated at the stern, the rear of my boat, which faced the parking lot. Unknown to me, a waiting insurance company PI took the opportunity to capture the entire event on film. I later thought about how I wished he could have been around to record all the weeks, months and years of me previous to that day. How immobile I was, in pain, and feeling tormented. Now that would have been worthy of his talents, but of course that's not why he was hired.

His skill was in his ability to capture that one 'moment of doubt' to be manipulated then used as some version of the definitive 'proof' of the fraudulence and hypocrisy of my claim of injury and, that could then be impressed upon the consciousness of all the various decision makers and other players, in this 'game' they ironically refer to as simply 'justice being served.'

Okay! I feel better now!

In actuality nothing of significance could really come from those few frames of photos, because they were merely but a snapshot or two of the whole, the bigger picture, which by now was meticulously documented in the endless piles of paperwork that comprised my injury claim.

But again, I've gotten a bit off track….

With plenty more research, I scouted out a nearly new propane-style heater as well as a propane cooktop. The problem was, as always, who would install these devices? A second more pressing issue which came to my attention via my neighbors was that if I insisted on using propane, a leak detention system would also be required. The complications inherent in my plans just kept surfacing, as well as the realisms of living on a boat were rife with the concerns of safety at every turn and at every stage of renovation.

Once during a particularly heavy rain-storm, I noticed that the boat seemed to be developing a slight list toward its bow, or front end. Eventually this listing became so apparent that I was moved to go outside and have a good look around. Once outside I could see nothing obvious, but after I stepping out onto the slick, rain-soaked dock, the source of the, what was by now severe listing, became obvious. The bow of my 'home' was slowly but steadily becoming submerged in the river. I was horrified!

After running around in a panic for what seemed like forever, I was at last able to settle myself down sufficiently enough to think things through. I determined that there was a bow-hatch, which was located in line with several water run-off channels, and it was these channels that had become clogged with debris. The subsequent backing up of all that rain water had nowhere else to go but down, through the lid of the forward hatch, into the storage compartment below where it progressively and rapidly grew in volume and weight!

Back inside my boat, I scrambled around rummaging through a little storage area which was crammed with clear plastic bins, to locate my submersible pump to use just for situations such as this one. Eventually, what seemed like much too long of time I had the pump plugged in the dockside power outlet, and lowered into the by now nearly six foot deep pool of accumulating water. At last, I could finally take a breath as water from the hatch began getting sucked out via the long fire hose attached to the pump. Soon the hatch was empty of water and my boat slowly righted itself.

I had become absolutely soaked through all my many layers of clothing and raingear. My feet, once removed from the soaking mass of socks in my boots, were a pasty pale white hue complete with multiple layers of overlapping skin-wrinkles. Once undressed and not until that moment did I recognise that I felt extremely cold and extremely exhausted.

After one very hot, but a little too short shower given the 6 gallon onboard hot water tank, I was head-to-toe pajamas and curled up in bed with my cats. The three of us were just a little traumatised, but what we couldn't know then was that this was just the beginning of something that, at times, would be a very interesting and difficult adventure.

Learning To Help Myself Again

By the end of April, which was about a month into my new boat-life, I became very frustrated waiting for someone to rescue me from my situation. I couldn't afford to pay for someone to install my nearly new propane heater, yet it had to be done. I was really suffering through the cold days, especially the wet, rainy nights and no amount of space heaters and heating pads was going to cut it. I felt desperate for answers until at last, one came.

My employment background was a mix of office work and outside construction jobs. I had received extensive telecommunications training in the areas of voice and data-network software systems, installations (primarily in telephone cable-splicing and telephone cable air-pressure systems), and some basic electrical, which all meant that I knew how to use tools and lots of them!

In fact anyone I had ever been with as a partner received their own little version of a tool box complete with all the basics that I thought they might need, and I trained them on their usage. This was something they could go to with confidence with or without me in their lives.

Out of what was abysmal gloominess came many ideas. More list-making ensued.

I meticulously planned out every aspect of the heater installation. I lay in bed at night thinking about it, and not until I felt certain that all the details were covered, would I even begin the task of installation. It took me many days just to get what I imagined were the right tools assembled for the job.

At long last I believed I was ready and carefully measured out the spot on the cabin wall where the heater was to be positioned.

However well prepared I thought I was, my powers to analyze and think things through by rational and logical processes now escaped me. The well-oiled machine that was my mind, the same one I used to call upon in situations just like the one I was presently confronted with, was not performing the way I imagined it should.

Every step of the way was fraught with confusion and indecision, and I would do one thing and only one thing at a time. I would get to the point in the install where a screw would be required to hold some part in place, but I got stuck on that; what size and type did I need? Which screwdriver and for what screw? What *was* I doing again? What *am* I doing?!

Every single item on the To Do List became a project of major proportions no matter how insignificant it was or, in my imagination at least, should have been.

For every 5 minute 'work' block I needed about 30 minutes of rest and recalculation time. I constantly referred to my 'plan of action' hoping to see some previously overlooked detail or word that might point the way to clarity and understanding. Ultimately these problem-solving cycles required more frequent longer episodes of recuperation for my brain to continue to function.

It took me about a week, but eventually, the heater was mounted onto its permanent place on the wall.

To say that this process was simply exhausting would be like describing your physical state as *just a little tired* after running a marathon. Constantly feeling exhausted meant all my time estimates ballooned into days and weeks from their initial calculations of minutes and hours. My spirits were quickly drained of their enthusiasm and yet I still hadn't managed to create an acceptable heating solution for my boat.

Asking For Help 101!

Before my injury I never ask anyone for help. I didn't know how to ask and I probably didn't believe that I needed to learn. Asking for someone else's help was the equivalent to admitting I didn't know something, which also meant that, according to my dysfunctional system of beliefs, that I was somehow a failure at being a person.

I thought that I always behaved appropriately humbled and vulnerable in certain, safe, situations. I could call a professional for advice, that was acceptable but to ask family or a friend for help that was my no-go, deal-breaker zone.

For several years prior to the accident I did get some intense exposure to my internal myriad of limiting self-beliefs and their tremendous impact on my life as a whole. There were the many ego-destroying self-awareness courses offered by my meditation and yoga group. All the work on myself I had done through the program of staying sober in AA. Then, a six week mind-body course fashioned directly from its parent course created by Author and PhD, Jon Kabat-Zinn from his bestselling book titled, 'Full Catastrophe Living.' All very useful and very consciousness expanding, so I thought I had done all the necessary work or at the very least the *worst* of it.

But despite all the hard work and all the tears it took to release the hurts and pain of my past for some inexplicable reason I could not bring myself to ask for help, from anyone (except for those things I deemed minor in nature).

Some wounds, it would appear, run deeper than others.

However I determined that was then, and this is now.

Those first few tentative steps towards asking felt so foreign and uncomfortable, but I did it anyway, I *had* to. One of neighbors, a very knowledgeable and capable sailor, came over to my boat one day and in less than two minutes had an eight inch vent hole bored through the roof of the cabin to accommodate the vent-pipe for my heater. Hallelujah!

The jubilant celebration that followed was only possible due to my forgetting of the million or so other details and steps that would need to be dealt with next!

I don't remember now exactly how much longer before I would actually have heat emanating out from the heater, many more weeks I'm sure but yes, eventually I did have heat. At the time it was glorious and soothing to my every bodily tissue, and even deeper still I was sure, down to my every molecule. The cats too seemed a bit more settled. Life was blissful again!

Something really great came out of the agony of not only having to rely on myself again, but taking the leap of faith to rely on others as well. Little by little, one belief at a time, I was re-cultivating the self-knowledge that had gotten me far in life.

Learning To Stand Up For Myself-Again

Soon, I was going to need as much confidence and belief that for me, was humanly possible. Judgement day was coming and soon, very soon, my life would be free of the insurance company's constant-probing tentacles, the profuse amounts of letters and counter letters from lawyers, the never-ending specialist appointments and worst of all an end to the, at times, debilitating anxiety and personal suffering, or so I thought then.

A few months prior to moving onto my boat I consulted, at the encouragement of my older sister, a tea-leaf reader. I had my tarot cards read a couple times in the distant past and honestly didn't remember but a few things of significance in those readings. But I become so distraught and I think too that

I felt very lost at the time so I'd figured then, why not give it a try?

I made the short ferry ride over to my sister's home on Vancouver Island where she and I made our way to a quaint heritage-style building that housed a little café where the 'Tea-Lady' plied her craft. After a cup of the obligatory tea and some uncomfortable chit-chat, something I used be proficient in, the reading began.

In the silence of the small cafe, I felt nervous and extremely fragile. After examining the remnants of my tea at the bottom of the cup, the tea-lady at last spoke, "this person that you've recently broken away from, the one that continues to cause you pain, you made it easy for *her* to hurt you. "

Huh?! Oh my God, she was referring to Katrina, how could she know that?! I said nothing; I couldn't speak because I just broke down sobbing.

I continued to cry throughout the entire reading, sniffling and snorting into my napkins, in this public place filled with people enjoying their tea and crumpets, I presumed.

Towards the end of the reading, she asked me to think of a question or a situation that I really needed an answer to or some guidance around but to ask in silence, only too myself.

I didn't have to think too long, I knew why I'd come to her in the first place; 'When was the insurance claim, also known as *The Nightmare*, going to end?! '

She sat for a minute or two then said simply "by the end of May". For the first time, in what I thought must be hours, I exhaled. I knew then, I was going to be okay.

I returned home feeling both rejuvenated and energized. The end was near.

CHAPTER X- THE END IS NOT THE ENDING.

May 2006-January 2007

"You will experience many setbacks in your recovery process because it is the nature of healing....Don't despair! These challenges, great though they may be, have arrived at precisely the right time to help you unfold and develop the particular strengths you need to realize the path back to yourself"- from Objects in the Mirror are Closer than they Appear.

Life progressed nicely for me after I received the tea-leaf revelation. I had a new neighbor, Ramona, a vegetarian like me. I had incorporated some dairy back into my diet in the form of cheese so was no longer, technically, vegan.

Ramona was a brilliant and very passionate Marine biologist doing some contract work in the area. She lived next to me with her cat Skooks, in a much too small, fiberglass sailboat that were both lovingly cared for by her. We were kindred spirits. For the first time in my recovery I connected with someone new, outside of the BI community, in a meaningful way that wasn't about neediness or dysfunction. We were just good friends, someone to have good talks with and the (more than) occasional rant too! She was also very funny and with a quick sense of wit. Her presence brought a whole new dimension of living literally right to my doorstep.

Having a support system like the one I had at the marina helped a long way in coping with the insurance claim battle I was enduring then. My boat-people family stepped in to assist at each turn regardless of the accompanying challenges, but in particular my good friends Butch and Carol, former dock neighbors, whose float home had been relocated up river the previous year.

Before they left though, their home located at the bottom of the dock-ramp, was C Dock-Central. If there was a barbeque happening it was there, including themed parties or just plain old social gatherings, this is where most of the (safe) action was. Their generosity and love was both the magnet and the glue that kept me, and many others, connected to them and the dock-community as a whole.

Butch had been shadowing me to the many appointments, playing multiple roles as safe driver and emotional support but more critically, he brought his reliable brain along too! He would remember the doctor's diagnosis, demeanor and any pertinent instructions whereas I could just basically show up because in reality that was pretty much all I *could* do.

His presence and support were huge then, and continue to be to this day.

John and Amy, who lived just a few boats away at the junction of two main fingers, shared many homemade waffle breakfasts and even more laughs with me and their various furry friends. There were other people coming and going as was the nature of a marina. Some came strictly on the weekends using their boats like quasi-summer lake houses while still others, curiosity seekers, poked their faces into our homes as one might at a boat show, at first startled to see someone inside, then would ask quite nonchalantly about a 'tour'. "It takes all kinds" we would often lament.

So it was with this tapestry of characters that I shared my life in all its incarnations and soon, when the proverbial 'shit' was about to hit the proverbial 'fan', it was these people who made it all utterly survivable.

The End Of (One Kind) Of Suffering

The end of May came and so too did the end of the (current) nightmare. Just as the tea-lady had predicted a few months prior, the insurance company settlement happened on

May 30, 2006.

I *was* free. No more harassment or nastiness coming thought the mailbox or over the phone lines in the form of legal motions, accusations and demands. All of that was over...except for the crying which came shortly thereafter.

As is often said, so much so in fact, that in reference to insurance settlements that it's fallen into cliché, "you never get what you expect to get", so consequently the tendency is *not* to believe it but *it is* true for most people. There are however, those rare persons who claim to have made a windfall, only what they deserved though, never revealing the dollar amount. And that's perfectly okay because anytime someone can get a proper and decent accounting, in terms of money value for their losses, in my opinion, is a good thing.

My ending did not feel like a good thing. The 'net gain', after lawyers' fees-33 1/3% (I also had to pay-off the first lawyer firm for their contributions), disbursements like miscellaneous and specialist opinion costs etc. and the other big one, reimbursement to several Health Insurance companies who had been paying my wages since the accident, what was *left* was mine- *negative* $5000.00!

Everyone took their piece of my pie, and didn't even have the decency to leave a single crumb, such is the system we all helped create then thrust our hopes and faith into, I bemoaned then.

I somehow regrouped out of the chaos and made a stand. I refused to sign-off until I got paid too. Some money would materialize, eventually, but it would take a little more time to manifest so until then, I continued to settle into boat-life and just keep going because what else was there to do?

Leaving it behind me- where it belongs...

I'm going to move on, for the most part, from the topic of Insurance Companies because the topic just doesn't merit any more space. This process consumed my life and deconstructed me to the point where I'm not willing to give it more of anything but quiet contemplation. I said only what I thought was important and relevant and that's enough for me.

My sincere wish is that you get out of this subject what *you'd* hoped to.

Finding Inner Strength

It was summer now, and I think the sun wore the hardest edges off the anguish I'd been carrying around both inwardly *and* outwardly. The time was right for a little vision-quest of a kind, so I made my lists of all the gear required then set off for a one week solo camping experience.

I hadn't camped for many years which meant that by that time I felt depleted of vital energy, sometimes referred to as spirit or intuitive-self, and my world desperately lacked the quiet reflection time so essential for the re-connection to its 'spirits' source. Other than the occasional tear-filled interruption from calls from lawyers, it was a glorious time.

Each night I would make a lovely fire and stare into it for hours. I was a little rusty at the camping experience, but I didn't care because out in nature I could be clumsy and forgetful and no one, except for me, was around to notice that the tent wasn't set-up quite right or that the pancakes weren't cooked through or that my camp-site looked like a bomb went off. It was awesome!

I spent most days staring into the river I had camped beside. One day I saw a mink swim across it then scramble deftly up the embankment disappearing into the dense bush across from where I sat. Now that was exciting!

I never felt bored, plus there were the countless hungry chipmunks with which to share my sunflower seeds. I went for walks along the river, cooked camp-food, was entertained by all the antics of the local wildlife, including the weekend human-variety and in general, began to de-stress from the previous 4+ years of personal struggle.

The night before I was to return home, I dug out all my journals that held all my deepest fears and craziest ramblings, and for the second time in as many years, committed them all to the fire. It was the perfect time to move on.

The summer before I had stopped off at this same site to rest before continuing on to my friend's house, that was a 2 hour drive, further on up the highway. By then I managed to drive, uninterrupted for an hour at a time then stop, rest and carry on for at least one more hour but by then I would be done. Not a kilometer more for the remainder of that day. While I was camped out in my car that night I had remembered to bring my current working journals and, as was my ritual, burned them as means of release to their tormented contents.

And now, I was entering a new phase of my life, put more aptly, re-entering this existence as a partially-reconnected whole person. I would have to reinvent my future since there wasn't going to be a fresh start in the form of a big payoff. As I packed-up my camp in preparation to return home, in my mind, I resolved to start dreaming again.

The Clarity Of Betrayal

Feeling betrayed would only go so far in my recommitment of a new life-plan and the residue of recent hardships brought an unexpected gift, clarity of thought. Another fog cleared, and this time it seemed as though I could see for miles, had I really come through it completely? That was unlikely, but life was a little brighter, and so, a little sweeter too, for now.

In October of that year, my dear friend Sheila lost her Mom suddenly. I was quite close to her family and had attended many functions including a few funerals in the past. I got a chance to see her Mom briefly before she passed, I only wished then that I could have been more present, but that would have required a healthy, uninjured brain, which I didn't have.

What this event offered up, quite unexpectedly, was the opportunity for me to be a friend again. Soon after her loss, I stayed with Sheila for a time during her transition through the pain of losing her Mom. I felt useful again.

This short but intense experience built up yet another, albeit very thin, layer of confidence and self-belief. A work in progress, yes, but that was preferable to the alternative, which was to be moving backwards or not at all.

While I was away tending to Sheila's needs, the cat-sitter I paid turned out to not be much of a cat person after all, but gratefully my neighbor Ramona stepped in just at the right time and took over caring for my neglected little furry ones.

I remember being quite hard on myself about the cats for a while. The old feelings of guilt, and the punishing thoughts that I was attracting the same old anguish-filled stuff I had become so good at attracting to myself. Luckily, Christmas brought some distraction when Butch and Carol threw the 'mother of all parties' which always served to help me forget about any current cat and financial troubles.

All that stuff quickly faded away completely, when January 2007 came, bringing a few big changes with it.

My settlement was revised and recalculated, when several health insurance companies at the urging of my lawyers allowed for my claim to be forgiven of certain monies owed by me, previously paid to me, while I was off work due to my injuries. It's complicated I know, but what it all meant was that I was going to get something after all.

I immediately paid the bills which were numerous. I had used credit to retrofit my living quarters to make it, to be blunt, livable.

As was the new pattern in my life there were several concurrent dramas playing out in their various forms. While I was helping care for Sheila, my poor cat, Martin had been ill and was getting sicker as each day passed. I was frustrated by what I reasoned were the vets' inability to find the root cause of it and my unwillingness and inability to pay for repetitive testing. This tension however motivated me to again stand up for myself and my 'dependant'. No one else was offering to do it. I made a few desperate phone calls to other vets and a veterinary hospital, until eventually, I found someone who listened to my growing concerns. As a result Martin was immediately admitted for care, and just in the nick of time.

Soon though, much bigger changes were in the air. Spring was around the corner and before I knew it, packing and moving, were once again the order of the day.

CHAPTER XI- Taking (Enormous) Risks

March-June 2007

"Another and much more treacherous type of False-Start is the one which springs upon you as a hopeful leap...you may be sparked by visions of yourself in a new and exotic role in life and strike out in search of ways to make this new role part of your emerging self"... From Objects in the Mirror are Closer than they Appear.

Handing a large lump sum of money to someone with a brain injury is a recipe for disaster. Unfortunately, I was no exception to this reality.

Having a good amount of cash at my disposal, more than I ever had before, at any one time, would prove to be very tricky indeed. That's not to say that I didn't make some very good, mostly fortuitous, decisions with it. I did, but the unfortunate part about these decisions was that they took me away from the very thing that kept me grounded and stable, my support system.

A (Gigantic) Leap Of Faith

I've never really considered myself a risk-taker, instead I've viewed all my big decisions as carefully considered and anchored in intuition; leaps of faith. The fact was however that this time and this decision *were* a huge gamble.

So it was with the assertion of my new self, to be more confident and bold but to above all, to take action. That's what brought about the huge decision to move. I reasoned it would be better to move, because to continue to live in a big city was out of the question.

My search was on for a new home. What started out in bliss-filled anticipation of greener and wider pastures got quickly downgraded to; "What can I afford, exactly?!", "Not much" came the reply!

It was deflating to realize that my options, although infinitely more abundant than they were just a few short weeks ago, were as I saw it then, very limited.

As time progressed I adjusted and readjusted my big dreams to be more congruent with a smaller, but perfectly adequate reality. Sheila lived closer to the towns that qualified as possibilities in my newly adjusted price range, and in short order with her help and guidance I found the proverbial diamond in the rough. The entire transaction took place over the phone and fax machine. The only picture I ever saw prior to buying was a blurry photo of the outside front-view of the house, which was also partially obscured by a large, but stunningly beautiful (I'd mentally noted) maple tree!

The financials took a few twists and turns, but ultimately the deal was done and soon, very soon I would be trying to figure out what it all really meant.

My former life has been a tremendous training ground for task completion challenges such as their organising and delegation followed by, the analyzing and compartmentalization of thoughts and ideas and problems into actionable steps. Probably I should think this explains my obsession with list making. I honestly can't help it, besides I reason, it works! Do what you know, so that's what I did then and continue to now, when a task calls for action which is their nature. I get to list-making.

It was with a bitter-sweet sadness to have to sell my boat, but somehow I was able to pass it along to kind and gentle man named Rene. I advertised it for sale in a free-ad service, and within a month or so it was sold. If you know anyone who has ever tried to sell their boat, then they will tell you that it was nothing short of a miracle as the process can typically take years…it was a sign I thought then, and a good one at that.

Where Did All This Stuff Come From?!!

How I acquired enough stuff to fill a 10ft x20ft (by 10ft high!) storage locker remains a mystery. I lived on a boat so, okay, many things had to be stored, but at some point I rented a second locker then, when that one became overfilled, I had emptied them both and crammed everything into a much larger unit. The unit I now needed to have emptied and packed into trucks, cars and a moving van, with the help of some very astonished, but devoted people.

The move required an all-out effort by my boat-people, TRG friend Debbie, good friend Sheila, and Kevin, a brain-injured family friend, Butch and his pick-up truck, an enormous moving van and my car (with small trailer in-tow)!

All organised, controlled and delegated by me, the least able in mind and body to pull it off, yet somehow, as it always seems to happen, things got done, people got fed, cats got crated and by the time the sun had nearly set, we got on our way.

Just a short few hours into my 'pilgrimage to a better life', the drive had become extremely treacherous. Sheila and I had taken turns driving my car while, Kevin my family friend who also acquired a brain injury a few short months prior to my own, navigated the moving van through a mountain pass during a lashing, all out snow storm. I didn't handle that kind of stress very well anymore. In actuality though, any level of stress could quickly wear through the thin veneer of my delicate coping mechanisms.

We'd managed to get out of the mountains safely and down into the glorious other-worldly looking valleys of vineyard lined hills and orchard clogged lowlands of the Okanagan Valley. We were almost there.

My new home was just another 90 minutes away, but our exhaustion prevented us from going any further. Sheila had left us and headed north to her home, her partner making the short trek down the highway to meet up with us and retrieve her. Kevin and I had then checked in to a motel, and quietly snuckin my two, equally exhausted cats.

I can clearly remember now how great I felt leaving the big city with all its hurts behind. I couldn't recall then, an earlier time where I felt so free and unencumbered, where life was good even though I had no clue as to what was really waiting for me at the end of the road. I later recognise this feeling as something familiar from my past. It was a sense of eternal optimism.

Okay, Where Do I Live Exactly?!

Driving into that little town with everything, every worldly possession and all my hopes and dreams felt like ten Christmases all wrapped-up into one gigantic moment of reveal. The climax though, the moment of truth, would just have to wait a few more minutes because I didn't actually know where I was going. The convoy of Kevin and myself came to a halt just inside the city limits, so I could frantically call Sheila for directions. Such a funny moment at the time, I could practically hear a band playing off in the distance, people cheering and celebrating, all that going on in my mind's eye, and as I spoke with Sheila, writing down her directions, the jubilant celebration simply dissolving into the ether.

As it turned out where we were parked was just a few minutes away from my 'fresh start'. Driving up that quaint street, *my street*, lined with 70's and 80's style one and two story homes all seemed just a bit surreal. To the left was a park, no actually it was a cemetery, "okay no problem" I thought, it looked like a park to me!

Then, there it was, better and more beautiful than I'd imagined and I couldn't believe my good fortune and became overwhelmed by the moment of truth. Kevin, however, just wanted to use the bathroom, and then get on with the colossal job of unloading.

After a quick walk through of my little palace, I settled the cats in one of the two bedrooms and gave them food and water, slid open a window, then left them to de-stress.

All I really wanted to do was get the sofa set-up so that I could then collapse onto it. I was already exhausted, but Kevin had other ideas. After several more hours, I was done. Kevin continued long after I'd given up. I was so grateful for his help, he was a moving and unpacking machine.

Kevin stayed on for another week, and did most of the work of getting me re-settled. He worked extremely hard and never complained about it, his commitment was incredible and I was really excited to share my new direction in life with at least one other person. We would sit outside in the front yard relaxing and marvelling at the spectacular unobstructed views of the grass covered hills, the antics of all the wildlife, the fresh crisp smells of nature but especially the continuous daily, hours upon hours, of sunshine. Now that was unbelievable!

Very soon after our arrival though, he was gone, and for the first time in a very long time, I was completely alone.

The Realities Of Isolation

Fortunately, I had a lot to keep me busy and the cats kept me company and entertained too. I hadn't realized how difficult it must have been for them living on the boat, trying to exist in an environment that constantly shifted under their feet. Here they were calmer, had fewer hairballs and illnesses, and were just in general a mirror image of me, happy and contented.

I kept enough money aside to cover the move plus address a few abysmal shortcomings in my little abode. The floors and window coverings were trashed and had to go. I'd brought all new-used appliances with me and with Kevin's tenacity they were already functioning as though they'd always been there.

The planning and preparation for the impending renovations, kept me occupied just enough to stave off the ever looming feelings of isolation and self-doubt.

Once my phone, internet and TV were up and running, I'd then have company of sorts, 24/7.

When did I become so afraid of being alone? I couldn't relate to myself, I'd never felt lonely before. It's was a strange thing, to feel alone and lonely when you're used to your life as being full of people such as strangers, friends and acquaintances and consequently filled with the noise of them and their activities, and then suddenly *nothing*. I was alone except for my thoughts, which were too numerous and clamoring to hold onto much less enjoy.

Days and weeks went by with me lying on the sofa, clicker in hand trying to recoup from all the frenzy of activity, and thought, leading up to the move. Lists and post-it notes littered the coffee table, computer desk and just about every other surface available that wasn't already taken up with a partially unpacked box.

I'd been getting to know the neighbors and probably talked way more than I listened and quickly wore most of them out with the incessant chatter. They were very polite though, and eventually I'd stopped telling them every little detail of my life. I just let the conversations roll out more organically, trying not to force them into a corner with all my stuff, which they *had* to know! It was hard to reel it in, even a little. I still felt very disconnected from myself most of the time and from those elusive social cues which for the most part continued to remain somewhat of an abstract concept. Still, I didn't let my odd communication style stop me from reaching out to strangers, but even taking those risks wouldn't be enough to sustain me.

My support network was more than 5oo kilometres away. What was I thinking?! My desperation, although not yet recognised as such, led me to an unexpected new friendship with Larry, the (new big screen) TV installer. We'd learned that we had some common career paths and at one point had even worked in the same building, at the same time, 10 years previously. His friendship proved to be a godsend of sorts.

By mid-June, the all the floors were done with new tile and new hardwood and they looked spectacular. The windows had new blinds, so privacy could now be claimed. All the doors, interior and exterior were replaced and a gaping hole in one of the outside walls that used to accommodate an A/C unit was transformed into, quite unexpectedly, a new window.

No sooner had the dust settled when I decided it was time for a road-trip. I packed up my cats, much to their great displeasure and headed back towards the Big City, the *former* bane of my existence. Once I was within a few short kilometres of the city limits, the familiar surroundings felt strangely, like home, only this time I was arriving as a visitor.

I needed to reconnect with my support-system, but didn't recognise my behaviour as such. I'd determined that, in the convolution of thoughts that is brain injury, this trip was a necessary evil in order to pick up much needed supplies. The drive was brutal. I honestly didn't think I was going to make it in one go, two or three seemed much more reasonable, and I made many unscheduled stops along the way hoping for a second wind to kick-in. None did. I'd resolved to stay in Vancouver long enough to regenerate myself sufficiently before making the dreaded trip back to my new home.

Once settled at Debbie's house I could relax. I had missed everyone terribly but still didn't understand the implications of it all. I socialized and bragged about my new home and pleaded with everyone to come and visit.

My inner energy source had been waning, and although I felt outwardly excited at the time, looking back it's clear that some major anxiety was already brewing.

I had a great time in Vancouver, and had dined out at all my favorite places for vegetarian, Hon's Won Ton House, All You Eat Sweets Indian Food and The Naam, with friends in tow. It was the big dose of love and acceptance, that without fully knowing it, I'd been so desperate for.

Once home, and only after another two weeks crashed out on the sofa, could I face the realities of housework, yard care and all the other endless things required to keep a household functioning. The weather became insufferably hot and I wasn't accustomed to back to back days of glaring, and by then, stiflingly intense sunshine and heat. I was astonished to see people outside walking their dogs and riding their bikes as if it were a pleasantly mild summer's day, complete with a gently blowing cool breeze. It wasn't anything like that, and I'd convinced myself that these people must somehow be immune to the heat!

By mid-July I'd had it. With all the labour, the suffocating heat but especially by now, with the severe loneliness. Something had to give, so my solution to everything was to hire a lawn care guy to deal with the lawn cutting stuff. Prior to moving I fantasized about mowing my lawn with my eco-friendly and sustainable electric mower, but the real life experience was nothing like the fantasy I'd spent hours contemplating. This was hard never-ending work and I'd be laid-up on the sofa constantly trying to recover from the mountains of To Do's, never quite getting to the state of feeling okay, not even close.

What appeared to be so unbearable for me to acknowledge, let alone address, was the idea that I'd made a colossal mistake, that in fact, this new life I'd chosen was completely unworkable and was an impossible dream or more accurately, insanity in action.

Reconnecting With My Intimate-Self

My new friend, Larry made the sting of loneliness a little more bearable. This new platonic connection was something I'd been sharing with my friends in the city and at one point while I was going on and on about him and all the things we were doing together, on the phone to my TRG friend, Debbie, she seemed a little too quiet. There was, for the first time ever in our conversations, a very long and very uncomfortable stretch of silence. The idea that she would abandon our friendship really frightened me. I needed this relationship of kindred's, like I needed oxygen. There was no one else I could relate to about being brain injured, and all of its inherent challenges, no one, in my mind, except her.

The present moment became an exercise in agony until at last, she spoke, haltingly at first, then getting her voice in order, she announced that she was attracted to me and was afraid to let the opportunity go by, and she would never forgive herself for not speaking up. I was quite honestly stunned by her confession. Where was this coming from and what was going on here, exactly?

The truth was that the attraction was mutual, but I'd kept it to myself in the hope that my feelings would dissolve, so that the friendship could continue. I didn't want the complications of a long-distance relationship, especially at a time where my loneliness was peaking. I knew my ability to make good choices was severely disabled and needed a complete make-over, but unfortunately our getting together was inevitable and to my delight, the streams of my imagination flowed with all things possible again.

What I couldn't know or wouldn't allow myself to see then, was what would eventually create an enormous mental and emotional fall-out for us both. The frequent and endless inconsistencies and contradictions that surrounded Debbie's life story were piling up in my subconscious.

PART II

CONFESSIONS OF AN ABUSER

CHAPTER I-Desperate + Lonely = (certain) Disaster

September 2007-May 2008

"I want your love, and I want your revenge
You and me could write a bad romance
I want your love, and all your love is revenge
You and me could write a bad romance"
Bad Romance by Lady Gaga

My romantic experiences five and half years post-accident had been nothing more than protracted nightmares; The Deli-Girl and Katrina and to a lesser degree Stella, my platonic travel-mate.

Despite their collective horrors I did learn from these experiences. I learned that I no longer had a 'thinking cap' or any other means of critical judgement, with which to sort through the myriad of facts one is confronted with, when making decisions about other people. But this is especially true when those other persons were being considered as potential romantic partners.

Unfortunately this deficit of knowledge did nothing to alter my behaviour and I continued to be incapable of making good choices and would inevitably pay a high price for playing with the matches of ignorance and dysfunction.

Life with Debbie started out bliss filled and very romantic. It was all great and I made several more trips back to Vancouver to see her, cats in tow. On one of these trips, less than six weeks into the coupling, we were involved in a car accident. It was the beginning of something so bleak, that perhaps if I had only paid closer attention to my reality, much of it could have been avoided.

I may never know for certain, but I believed this to be so, and thus clung to that moment as the Rubicon in the relationship, the moment that I could have walked away, but didn't.

Who Is This Person?!

Debbie and I had been friends for 5 years and close friends for about two of those. She was always very private and protected her personal information closely. Since I did most of the talking during this time it boded well for her not to have to talk too much and thus she kept her private life intact, which then allowed me the time and space to blab effortlessly and continually.

To some people, *the truth* is viewed as a flexible and malleable concept. Debbie was one of those people.

Philosophically, I believe that some truths are a temporary state. This meaning any given set of facts can be true in that moment, but once new information comes to light, then this new, *integrated* statement, becomes the *truth*. I've learned that we all come with our own unique statement of truths, some bending to fit the situation, while others steadfastly unyielding to no-thing.

My perception of reality was handicapped, which meant that while Debbie appeared to have unlimited energy and ability to bend and manipulate her truths, I had limited tools with which to interpret her 'facts'. So, our life together from its beginnings was rife with confusion, misunderstandings and the ensuing frustration that all of this insanity created. I'd soon recognise too that Debbie didn't really pursue an active life but rather a cerebral one.

Unfortunately the recent car accident put us both back in terms of physical and cognitive recovery. In the accident, my head had been violently whipped from side to side, and my brain was once again scrambled. Debbie was driving at the time and got the worst of it as we, and the car we were in was

T-boned at an intersection by another driver running a red light.

Once at the hospital emergency, Debbie strapped into a gurney, and me on foot next to her, I could see the beginnings of something I didn't think I really wanted to be a part of.

The intake person began asking the various vital questions, directed towards Debbie, and in a loud voice, which was practically yelling, could be heard from her location about ten feet away behind the reception window.

"Are you taking any prescription medications right now?"

As I stood next to Debbie, pondering my own aches and pains and wondering too about the inevitable series of physical therapies that I would soon become engaged in, she began to give an accounting of her list of necessary medications.

I wasn't really paying attention at first, until it occurred to me that the list of drugs she was ingesting was going on and on, and at the time, seemingly endless. I recognised only but a few of the names, the ones similar to what I was taking but the rest just sounded just plain scary.

I had continued to manage my own symptoms with the two medications that had been prescribed for me since my time at GF Strong. One for, what were generalized severe aches and pains categorized as fibromyalgia just the previous year, and the other to address poor sleep patterns and neurologic pain, due to the brain injury.

These drugs, I could understand their purpose, but with Debbie's recital of each new drug name including their applicable dosage, my anxiety grew, and so too the realization that I didn't really know this person, at all. Some drugs had more ominous sounding names than others, but it was the totality of them combined, that they were a force to be reckoned with. The subsequent fear this created in me caused me to feel even more ill. The total sum of the situation was alarming and destabilizing. It was impossible to take in all at once.

With Debbie's car trashed, I made the long, lonely trek

back to her place to retrieve my car. As I sat on the bus on route back to her apartment I knew then that I was in shock. My head hurt, as did the act of thinking, and I felt devastated by this new reality I would soon be faced with. In my mind this new relationship had all the hallmarks of a disaster in waiting.

After seeing the look on Debbie's face a few minutes after the impact, I had already sensed that a victim identity was emerging. Her expression then reminded me of a small child's upon losing their ice-cream off the top of their cone, simply devastated. She was frozen with it, and needed to be taken care of. Not to understate the seriousness of the accident, but we both walked away from it and things could have been much, much worse. Yes, there were some long-standing fallout issues, such as greater fatigue and even more body pain, but we were both accustomed to having to deal with stuff like that.

This was more about the *heartbreak of setback* to one's current ongoing progress than all the physical manifestations put together. The long and difficult road of rehabilitation starts anew, regardless of one's state of readiness.

I'd considered the idea that I could just leave, just be a good friend to her, I was good at that. It was a valid option, and I had spent a lot of time thinking about it before returning to the hospital to collect Debbie. But with my brain scrambled and hurting, I just couldn't hang on to any concepts for long however, no matter how critical they were to my well-being.

By the time I'd gotten back to retrieve Debbie, my guilt-riddled self would not allow me to do what I'd reasoned by then was tantamount to abandonment. Adding to the current complications of my damaged-self, was my overriding belief that I still needed to needed and could not be okay *and* be alone.

In A Relationship, But Still Alone

The next few months were excruciating examples of how the small seed of frustration and invalidation can morph into the more difficult condition of feeling deep resentment. Debbie came to visit on several occasions, staying for increasingly longer intervals. During these visits, she slept practically around the clock, getting up only at my urgings to eat or bathe or both. Our intimacy levels while initially healthy, rapidly declined, and showed some early indications of dysfunction.

By November, she was getting between 5 and ten different types of therapy sessions per week, but her overall health seemed to be on the decline. Our phone calls were a confusing mix of repetitive comments, mostly from me, attempting to sense that she had grasped at least part of the conversation. Debbie was just not there, and her own descriptions of things seemed highly unreliable to me. She wasn't ever truly present at any one time, but in my mind this was really just an exaggeration of her state prior to the accident.

In December, she came and stayed until sometime in January, and it was during this lengthy stay that I suggested to her that she could come and live with me permanently, so I could better keep an eye on her and her rehabilitation. Just prior to the accident in September, she had been attempting to get her condo listed for sale, so she too could move to out of what was in her own words, something akin to the hostile and unforgiving energy of the big city.

Several more months later, and after a few more back and forth trips and she was moved in, for better or for worse, I convinced myself. Her condo sold just on the heels of the major real estate meltdown, luck was on our side, or so we chose to look at these events that way at the time.

Of course I became very worried. The packing and moving of her things proved to be the beginning of my eventual emotional and mental undoing. I hadn't recognised the profuse amount of evidence in her home for what it really was, the warning signs and symptoms of a hoarder.

I have to qualify that last statement as mine, and the opinions of some health professional friends of mine, Debbie's behaviour was never officially categorized this way by any physician or other professional in the field of OCD-Hoarding.

That being said, I believe that her living habits were obsessive and compulsive in nature to the point where she was unable to complete most tasks in a timely matter, regardless of their simplicity. For me attempting to deal with this reality became frustrating in the extreme. Nothing in my coping set of tools could adapt to the challenges of her convoluted thinking patterns of complex rationalizations. She *was,* the often over-used but proverbial, conundrum wrapped in an enigma, and I was quite clearly out of my league.

At an earlier point in time, and after we'd had a falling out due to yet another confusing story, where the 'facts' just weren't adding up, I'd allowed myself to believe things as the truth that I had known then, were false. I consciously made the decision to continue in the relationship, despite seeing a boatload of red flags.

Loneliness might well be ranked in the same category as stealing in some circles of thought. It is that distasteful for the mind to acknowledge, and this was doubly true for me.

CHAPTER II-THE CHAOS BEFORE THE STORM

June -August 2008

"Fear is sometimes called the source of all our negative emotions...Fear has a way of preying on a single aspect of loss by taking over your life with a specific dread. It can paralyze your progress but is really, as an emotion of grief, trying to lift your burden of loss through helping you to know yourself better."...Objects in the Mirror are Closer than they Appear.

Soon after beginning our life together as a co-habiting couple, the chaos had quickly begun to ramp up around us. My little home was adequate for two functioning adults, which we clearly did not yet qualify as.

The two bedroom bungalow with garage, cute with a semi-manageable nine hundred square foot interior, was just about all I could handle on my own. Most days I didn't really manage too much other than cooking meals, pet care and sweeping up the cat-litter covered-tiled floors.

I always thought that it was a plentiful house for us but not for Debbie, she constantly maligned its small size and lack of space for all her things. She preferred large furniture, which was never going to work in this tiny abode. I sympathized with her, and was aware of her growing anxiety over not being able to settle in without having the many reminders of her life around, meaning all the *things* she was used to having around.

Within a few days of her permanent re-settling, we were on the hunt for the perfect home. We had done some looking previous to her move, but I had lost most of my motivation to continue, and assumed she had as well. Not so, she was more determined than ever and I quickly grew tired of the many viewings and promising leads in our quest for a forever, *home of our dreams*.

By mid-May, I asked that we postpone the search so I could get some much needed R & R. Summer was coming, the birds were back and my little yard was the perfect bird-watching venue. The relaxation period lasted for a few weeks all the while punctuated by Debbie's cries of, "Oh my God, come and see this one!" or "this one looks so beautiful!" She was spending most of her waking hours glued to the computer, scouring through endless pages of real estate listings.

I felt absolutely worn out and worn down, so I decided to put away my protests and re-commence the search, despite my growing sense of dread and feelings of what were by now, deep resentment.

Within a short time of reluctant searching the perfect, forever home was located but before any relocating was to occur our current home required some intense cleaning. The spare room had become Debbie's dumping ground for all the chaotic projects that swirled around her constantly. Her pet bird was practically lost among the many piles of partially unpacked boxes, stacks of paper and piles of dirty clothing, dirty dishes, bird droppings and seed remnants, a disaster zone both visually and fragrantly.

I was horrified by it all, but incapable of staying within my feelings for very long, so instead I got to work cleaning and fixing the situation. When in times of distress, I often defaulted to my most comfortable coping strategy, which was *rescuing others from their own chaos and making it my own*.

The War Of Attrition Has Begun

One of Debbie's more ingrained coping mechanisms was to ponder and agonize over every detail, no matter how small or how insignificant, of every possibility or situation requiring a decision. I had allowed this behaviour to slowly, but inevitably, erode my defenses to the point where an emotional explosion was imminent. The day finally came when I was over-the-top yelling and raging about the apparent stale-mate she had reached in her process of decision-making. She had wanted the new house, obsessed about it, was in love with it, but chose instead to sit in the spare room/office locked in a battle with her thoughts. She wasn't progressing closer to a decision, at least as far as I was concerned.

The fact was she needed that time to meticulously go through every fear and every doubt that sprung from her mind. She had to give the situation all her focused attention in order to feel assured of her choices. That took time, a lot of time, but I no longer had any patience for her processes and had reached my limits of tolerance of what I viewed as her procrastination and indecision. I eventually erupted in a tirade of nastiness that I'd known was coming but felt justifiably angry until, I didn't, and then I just felt awful and guilt-riddled about my behaviour.

Contained within this episode of grief-expressed-as-fear, a familiar relationship pattern in my life had begun to re-establish itself;

Victimhood mindset (Debbie) + Need to Rescue (Michelle) + Persecutor Complex (Debbie & Michelle) = The Trifecta equation of dysfunctional and toxic collaboration!

Trying To Get Help In A Small Town

Isolation from our friends and family was now more than ever apparent in our inability to sort through our collective difficulties. With my support system cut-off, I chose to reach out to the local mental health ministry for help. There I'd received some excellent counselling from someone who quickly and efficiently helped me get to crux of my situation; brain injury + lack of understanding and coping + absentee partner = frustration. I also needed to examine my growing resentments, which added fuel to the fire of the greater (insidious) issue of lack of trust. Unfortunately this help wouldn't last, as my counsellor soon moved on to a new opportunity elsewhere in the province.

Had I continued with another counsellor, perhaps the rage brewing beneath the surface of paper thin walls of my cool exterior, would not have punched through in such short order. I'd hadn't continued because I'd somehow convinced myself that Debbie and I were just over-stressed and under rested and that our partnership could handle the current few bumps in the road.

There was something else that came out of the brief experience with the counsellor I was seeing. This was the realization that both Debbie and I were somewhat damaged beings, from our collective childhood and other life dramas and that we'd both brought all that baggage with us, and, so to the inability to sort through any of it with my brain-damaged thinking and her altered state of a severely drugged brain. Complicating matters further was the ever present massive amounts of free-floating anxiety swirling around us both.

Brain-Injury Part II

The lasting effects of the most recent car accident, now nearly 10 months on, continued to make our communal lives uncomfortable. I regressed on nearly every level of rehabilitation; my words and their associated comprehension were once again lost to me, the crippling exhaustion remained chronic, my mental and emotional states weren't stable and in real danger of slipping further.

At the time though, I thought that I was only *mildly* stressed, my powers of rationalization working overtime, to meet the high demands of a crazy-making situation.

It was so disheartening to me at the time, each day having to relearn things and re-commit to getting better. It was a long and tough period punctuated by many very poor decisions being made, then unmade, then remade again, a very crazy time in hindsight.

A few close friends often talked me out of even more radical ideas, like the one where I suggested that Debbie and I should get married, as soon as possible! The idea is obviously irrational now, but back then *nothing* made any sense, and I was simply stumbling my way through my life with one horrendous choice after another. The consequences of which, would show up in some solidified form, such as buying a new, much bigger home, while at the same time being completely incapable of managing the current, much smaller one. "Just one more example of brain injury in action," I'd often be fond of saying.

On The Move-Again

I cannot remember any other time in my past where I was so uninspired to pack and move. Yes, in the past I'd been paralyzed with indecision and fear, and also too, frozen in my earlier state of perplexity, not knowing what to do next. Those episodes aside, my usual frame of mind would be pumped with the anticipation of new beginnings, but not this time, this was different. Instead it became a time of sadness, I was abandoning my Fresh Start and wasn't anywhere near ready to say goodbye to it.

The chore of packing was not as bad as it could have been, if were not for the fact that I hadn't fully unpacked, and most of Debbie's belongings were already packed, ready and waiting in storage.

My lone new-friend Larry and current family friend Kevin, who had decided to return from the city to take care of my little house, pretty much took care of the momentous move for Debbie and me. Her things had been waiting patiently for their liberation from an isolated storage facility located near to town. It was 40C the day we moved, absolutely gross weather for practically anything, except for the local pastime, tubing down one of several local pristine rivers.

The decision not to sell my little home was one born out of deep resistance to letting it go. I'd also rationalized, privately, that if things between Debbie and me continued to go sideways, worse than they already were, I'd always have a safe haven to retreat to. So, I hung onto it, never imagining then, the depth and breadth of personal hells, which could and would eventually materialize.

CHAPTER III-HARDSHIPS AND REALITY-CHECKS

September -December 2008

"Denial is as tricky as it is helpful because, like numbness, it can lure you into a false sense of well-being and fool you into not being realistic about your condition. This can create great physical or emotional problems, as you attempt to go about acting like a completely functional person without the ability to do so."...from Objects in the Mirror are Closer than they Appear.

The 'big-house' and the accompanying acreage it rested upon were an incredible alchemy of a beautifully constructed post and beam dwelling in perfect balance within the backdrop of resplendent nature. It was one of the most magnificent and tranquil properties I'd ever laid eyes on and I only wish now that I could have been better able to fully appreciate all its gifts and splendour.

Without the ability to be fully aware or make half-descent decisions, we'd just invited numerous mammoth learning curves into our lives, all of them requiring action on every level of thought and physicality, one could possibly imagine. Once moved in, the splendour of our new abode would soon fade replaced by the realities that only doing hard labour could bring.

After getting some expert advice we opted to do several necessary repairs and adjustments to the house in order to make it more heat efficient. This ultimately eroded a good deal of Debbie's savings, but it was planned for and expected, unfortunately her security levels plummeted paralleling her dipping bank account.

We had a plan but it became obvious later that it was extremely convoluted, making it impossible to follow or reconcile any investments. We'd assumed then that we would be living there until something better, in the distant future, caught our attention. This was our forever-home for now so the investment was worth it, which was how we'd approached the spending around the repairs and necessary alterations. Unfortunately, staying on a budget was no longer one of my strong points and with Debbie essentially out-of-it cognitively, most of the time, the responsibility to do mountain of chores fell on my shoulders, exclusively.

Very soon into our life of happily-ever-after, the cracks that had been born of earlier strife rapidly grew into crevice dimensions. The war which had been brewing now erupted and any issue that was remotely contentious became an all-out battle of low-blows and pot-shots. Of course I realized too that most of these fights were, in the early going, only one-person attended as Debbie was simply mentally, emotionally and physically absent and unavailable most of the time.

In the spirit of what was our collective insanity, we deemed it the perfect time to rescue a badly abused and neglected dog. She was in terrible condition which improved ever only slightly throughout the course of her brief existence. We'd reasoned then that what she needed we could provide, and so we soon had another mouth to feed, one that also needed a drawer filled with prescription drugs in order to keep her afloat too. A perfect fit to our growing menagerie of cats and bird, not to forget the many dozens of outside critters, benefactors of endless handouts of seeds and nuts!

I shake my head now, as I write these words because we were so unwell then on every level imaginable but we were doing our best, however, that was never going to be adequate enough under those circumstances.

The (Not So) Simple Life

The exhausting work of firewood-gathering and splitting commenced alongside the daily chores of cooking, feeding and cleaning-up after everyone, furry critters included. My patience worn thin, and I no longer made requests or sugar coated things, as our situation demanded participation from everyone.

My typical daily routine began at 7am and ended with me collapsing into bed around, if the planets were aligned and all the pets had behaved- 11:00 pm- delirious with exhaustion. Debbie's unique schedule, on the other hand began usually around 1pm when she seemed able to drag her drugged-self out of bed and contemplate the day for generally no more than a few hours, long enough to take her daily, copious amounts of medications, eat, watch TV then back to the comforts of bed.

I didn't have but a small understanding of depression then, one would think that by that time I would have, but I didn't. Perhaps if I'd been able to admit to my own feelings of depression and despair earlier in my life, the subsequent ignorance levels created out of the *fear of being depressed,* could have been lowered significantly.

The truth was that I was hurting too. I had continued to grapple with all the side-effects of another brain-injury and the increase in physical pain. Debbie's coping strategies differed from mine. I got busy with getting well which meant keeping my body strong and maintaining good nutrition and other positive living habits. Her positive living habits were not as ingrained or practiced as mine and she didn't have the benefit of more than a decade and a half of disciplined living, like I did.

Her coping mechanisms manifested most often as isolation and withdrawal from life, depression and severe anxiety and the denial of her immediate reality. These were her primary go-to behaviours in times of stress, and whenever extreme stress was present, her coping strategies would then match up in severity with her perceived reality.

We were quite the pair!

Winter was coming. When I was still in the small house, I'd enjoyed my first small town winter experience immensely. I would shovel the small driveway of snow in mere minutes and love taking in the fresh clean air. I'd go for walks stopping to chat with neighbors and strangers along the route. Funny thing about small towns I'd noticed is that no one really feels like a stranger, but rather like extensions of the neighborhood. Everyone belonged everywhere and no one was out of place. Not like life in the city where, if you found yourself lost or in the 'wrong' part of town you knew it and would rectify it immediately by getting out of there a.s.a.p., before someone reminded you of that fact, sometimes with unpleasant consequences.

Not so in my little town, where life *was* simpler but not necessarily easier. I wasn't managing my life very well then either, but that aside I didn't have to confront then what I was now faced with. The bleak reality was that we, Debbie and I, were going to have to learn several back-the-land living principles soon, or we'd rapidly succumb to the harshness of the situation.

Gone was the luxury of turning up the thermostat at will, the five minute shovelling of snow, the bliss filled walks in quaint neighborhoods, the short walk to shopping and all other necessities this was the highly-touted, highly fabled life of *living in the bush*.

The Fires Of Peri-Menopause

I'd believed for years that I was somehow immune to all those awful, legendary tales of horror, one would often hear regarding what was for many middle-aged women, something innocuously described as, *the change of life*.

In my opinion, it was a terrible and excruciatingly obvious humourless-joke, perpetrated on the global masses of unsuspecting females, now that I believe, would come a just bit closer to the reality.

I hadn't a clue about what was lurking around the corner, and about to befall me then. Even though I'd had done a lot of reading on the subject of peri-menopause and had numerous friends who'd begun their own change-of-life journeys, I'd inexplicably remained unprepared for my own. That all changed in a hurry.

Soon, and without my being aware of the warning signs, my sleep patterns already disabled by brain injury were further assaulted by the unrelenting advancement of age, and it's resulting biological hormonal changes. All semblance of sleep came to a screeching halt. My nights were filled with the unforgiving heat of an internal fire-that was hot flushes; my body perspiring in the extreme in an effort to cool and counter stabilize the hormonal imbalance battles that were raging on inside my brain and body, like a chemistry experiment gone awry.

The resulting sleep deprivation paired with its consequence, irritability, further fueled by the seeds of rage within me, created a perfect storm of mental and emotional wrath, destruction and doom!

But I'm getting a little ahead of myself...this end-result state-of-being from my-change-of-life reality, more accurately, was greatly exaggerated by other factors. There was the slow but deliberate process of character dismantling, sustained physical hardship and finally, the emotional and mental fall-out from lack of validation and support (which ultimately lead to the depletion of all my coping resources). This totality combined, lead to my inevitable undoing.

CHAPTER IV-DESCENT INTO (COLLECTIVE) HELL.

December 2008-February 2009

"Anger...is overlooked as a healthy expression of grief. With a brain injury...what might have previously registered as displeasure with a frustrating task, or situation, has now become a battleground for your fight to comprehend and control your world." From Objects in the Mirror are Closer that than Appear

My Daily To-Do List continued to grow both in length and breadth. At first, just having more responsibilities gave me a greater sense of purpose and, I believed then, that this new feeling would eventually restore me to my former state of *well-being*. I'd hung on to this philosophy grasping tightly with the understanding too that I'd need to recommit to it daily.

My prevailing attitude at the time was that hardships played a vital role in personal growth, which can lead to one's eventual transformation. Sounded great but in reality I'd often think, "One can only handle so much transformation at any given time!"- And by then I'd already reached my adversity saturation point.

There have been times in my life where I was sure I was being punished for past transgressions...this was one such time. Every difficulty, no matter how insignificant it may have been, threatened my mind's tenuous link to optimism.

My life did not exist outside of the lists of daily tasks, which served to only further nurse the underlying preoccupation that I was not worthy of happiness.

I Don't Think I'm Cut-Out For This After All!

The snow started to fall and accumulate in early December 2008. I thought I was prepared and had the plow blade attached to the ATV (this task took nearly a week and had me reduced to a trucker-mouth, trash-talking maniac in no time!).

Snow-plowing, which started out as novel and fun, was quickly downgraded to a chore and a huge drag. I rapidly began to feel dread at the slightest hint of snowfall, and winter had become for me, what it already was for the multitudes suffering with SAD (seasonal affective disorder); bleakness times 100!

But snow-plowing was a science, and I decided that like everything else it just required a little focus and understanding. Unfortunately, I was no longer very adept at either of these, and my frustration levels were going to peak very soon.

During this time, Debbie and I had developed a friendship with an older couple who offered to teach us a few things about plowing and wood gathering. Their help was invaluable as it back-filled some of the many knowledge gaps I'd been struggling with. Our friendship with them was only temporary, but I was forever grateful to them for those few little nuggets of wisdom. The sad part was that they'd left us with some pricey ATV and chainsaw repairs so things had ended rather poorly between us.

For me that experience, of our friends wrecking things, and not paying for the subsequent damages (which I characterized then, as betrayal) marked the beginning of a long and painful period of what I now refer to as *The Customer Service Wars*! Predictably, I engaged in a lot more misery before I was truly battle-ready!

Snow-removal was just one of the many physically challenging requirements of the 'simple life'. There were also the many physically demanding aspects of firewood preparation, the equivalent of a small-time logging operation, the felling of dead trees, collecting and dragging logs back to a central prep-area, cutting up logs into precision length rounds, then splitting and stacking them into strategic piles, and finally, loading up 2-3 weeks' worth of prepared wood to stack next to the house for immediate use.

All of this activity took a huge toll on our bodies, and hampered to some degree, proper healing of some old and a few recent injuries. Mentally and emotionally, I would be spent at the end of my first firewood season. I'd actually demanded that Debbie get dressed, and participate in the wood-splitting session that would last three solid days. I'd already been giving her several early warnings and drop strong hints as the weekend of the wood-splitter rental approached.

She grudgingly joined me in this gruelling task, eventually though she got into it and actually began to perk-up as a result of doing something other than sleeping and zoning out. She'd even hinted at the prospects of feeling useful again but, unfortunately I'd no time for her graduated, return-to-the-land-of-living recovery plan. I needed her to show up every day, and thus started to make more frequent demands on her time commitment to our new life, the one we both literally signed up for.

By January, my plowing prowess went a long way towards me feeling less burdened by the snowfall. However, nothing seemed to address my frequent, loud and aggressive ranting's that were by then, a regular daily occurrence in the household.

Our budget continually took a beating with the many endless, unexpected costs of repairs, rentals and occasional impulse purchases all conspiring to undermine our carefully laid plans. Plans that made it possible for us to believe we could pull off this crazy idea to begin with. Debbie used up a sizable portion of our combined income too, for her many frequent necessary therapies and only after much discussion would she grudgingly agree to drop one or two per month. Our lives became nearly 100 percent focussed on her issues of poor health, poor nutrition and practically non-existent self-care. There seemed to be never any time for my needs, and I seldom had the time, energy or fiscal freedom to add any maintenance therapies to my own life.

I felt as if I existed solely for the purpose of manifesting her aspirations of having a better life for herself, and only for her. My needs didn't appear to be factored in anywhere, in this noble endeavour.

How A Promise Became A Pact Of Silence

Back in 2007, when I made that, fate-filled, decision to stay with Debbie, it was with the promise that she would seek immediate counselling for some long-standing toxic behaviours, in particular, those which threatened the health and integrity of our relationship. She'd kept her promise but somehow, under the guise of seeking help, her issues were repurposed as strategies to protect her from what was commonly referred to as my controlling tendencies.

In fairness to everyone involved at the time, I *was* controlling and my own toxic behaviours created tremendous relationship difficulties, on top of what was already a very difficult time. The fights generally started with my accusations voiced in anger, then, Debbie's passive-aggressive tactics kicking-in thus triggering my persecutor persona in the extreme. Our lives became a war-zone. We were in constant attack and defend mode, and peace-treaties while agreed to in principle, couldn't last under the seismic pressures of expectation and resentment.

What happened next was the eventual result of all these things, including my perception of an ongoing conspiracy of sorts, which culminated in the eventual complete deconstruction of my character.

I had it with being identified as *the problem*. There was seldom any communication between us regarding her counselling, now nearly 2 years on, and as her partner, I hadn't ever been invited to join in the process of co-facilitation of the shoring-up or our relationship. I'd felt like a complete outsider, the enemy and not to be trusted.

It all came to a head one day, as Debbie and I were trying

to discuss the many issues we couldn't seem to ever come to common ground on. As was the pattern with our 'discussions', my voice getting increasingly more and more stressed then, rising in volume and menace, until its eventual crescendo of practically shouting out a long litany of accusations followed by their corresponding demands.

Suddenly, and without any warning Debbie blurted out, "My counsellor says that you are abusive, manipulative and controlling!"

Silence.

I sat there stunned. My brain throbbing from those three, hard, sucker-punches to the head.

In the space of just a few moments those three words filtered their way down into my consciousness, and I came to the obvious conclusion that they were, in fact, the truth. Then, in a calm voice, I simply said, "Your counsellor is absolutely right." Pause. "This is why we need to break-up. You need to be with someone different, and so do I."

I remember clearly the next scene, as Debbie's jaw dropped to the floor and I had quietly gotten up from my chair and left the room. As unbelievable as this may seem, I don't believe that either of us saw that one coming.

CHAPTER V-ALONE *AND* ISOLATED

March 2009-December 2010

"We act out because, ironically, we think it will bring us some relief...Then the nightmare gets worse...When you get to tell someone off, you might feel pretty good for a while, but somehow the sense of righteous indignation grows, and it hurts you. It's as if you pick-up hot coals and throw them at your enemy. If the coals happen to hit him, he will be hurt. But in the meantime you are guaranteed to be burned." From, Start Where You Are, by Pema Chadron.

A very big decision came out of the break-up confrontation. Just into the sixth month of happily-ever-after, we decided to list the house for sale, and move on from the relationship.

The next few months were filled with all those activities one is obliged to do when attempting to sell their home, and just a few short weeks after listing, we thought, according to our realtor, we'd hooked a proper buyer. We got to the business of separating assets then packing and storing them in preparation for our new, separated life paths.

It was a crazy couple of months of back and forth negotiations of dates, where the buyer needed more time to secure financing and prepare for all the typical inspection requirements. During that time our realtor turned away other prospective buyers, insisting the deal was done...unfortunately though, it was not done.

We were devastated when the deal eventually imploded, as we'd had everything, especially our sanity, riding on it; new beginnings and fresh starts sure, but most necessary at that point was getting as far away as was possible from one another.

What remained of the listing season, in a small economically decimated market were really only a few more pockets of opportunity. A week here and there aligned with specific other events, such as when kids had returned to school and prospective buyers would be back house hunting for a brief time before getting ready for the winter holidays.

We were getting viewings but with each rejection came a deeper, inner rejection creating more and more abysmal grief. It was exhausting and spirit deflating and soon we would be confronted by the prospect of another 'winter of discontent'.

The Customer Service Wars, A Continuing Saga.

It was with this backdrop of grief, frustration and discontentment that my attitude took on ever increasingly dark and bleak outlook. I'd often think about how horrible my life predicament was, and note that I would never have to remain somewhere I didn't want to be. I'd always been free to pack up and leave whenever I chose to, but not now, I was firmly stuck in what felt like a cavernous sized rut.

It's comical now, and with a sense of irony that only hindsight can bring, to reflect back on all the ongoing simultaneous product and service difficulties I was dealing with that appeared to spring up endlessly during that time. I could not then, it seemed, be capable of purchasing anything that didn't eventually turn out to be defective or outright broken.

These *Customer Service Wars* manifested as constant daily battles between me and the many customer service contact persons of their respective corporations. Mostly, these companies were giant conglomerates, which only served to feed my already enormous sense of feeling persecuted and hard done by. I had become an extreme victim of sorts; the world *was* out to get me. Under these circumstances, my feelings of anger, and what were by now an infinite number of resentments simply continued to multiply.

A Very Close Call

I'd be reminded daily of the parallels to my experience in recent times with the legal system. To me it was the same old same old, how had I gotten myself into such a horrid mess? I'd spent my days raging at the world, and my nights crying while shaking my fists at the same cruel world. I'd become hopeless.

This was a dark and miserable period in my life that nearly did kill me. I'd honestly thought I wasn't going to get through it. This awful cloud, that followed me everywhere and blanketed my every thought with darkness, came to a dramatic conclusion of sorts one day, while I was driving into town to see my family doctor.

The route into town was a 10 minute scenic drive complete with spectacular views of the rolling hills of ponderosa pine punctuated by areas of grassland range. It should have been beauty to the eye of any beholder but not to me, not then. It was with tears streaming down my face, as I approached a sharp corner that bent hard to the left, where I considered the idea of just driving off the edge. It would be quick, I imagined then.

I just barely stopped myself from going through with the hastily conceived plan, because I reasoned that if I died, Debbie would get everything, and that my friends and family and my beloved little cats would get nothing. It was too much for me to bear, so I chose instead, to continue to live. This was the second time in my life where resentments actually kept me *alive*.

The one other occasion where I could honesty admit that my rage, partnered with despair, kept me going during that awful stretch of insurance company harassment.

T'is Better To Be Labeled A Victim Than An Abuser...

As my behaviour became increasingly aggressive and erratic, I reasoned that no one would really want to be around me, or have anything to do with me because I had become that miserable, inside and out.

I tried to get some counselling, but the ministry had determined that after two visits to see someone, one more than was recommended, I did not qualify for more assistance. If I had only said that I was being abused or severely depressed or had out of control drinking, I could have gotten much more help. I didn't say these things because I didn't feel any of these things. I felt homicidal.

I'd come to understand through my somewhat twisted perspective, that there was no help for those of us labelled *Abusers*. If I'd been a victim of abuse, as Debbie maintained she was, and to some degree that was true, I would have had heaps of resources offered to me, as she in fact did.

After this experience, I became even more resentful, but ironically, eventually this grave state of mind gave rise to a philosophy that both surprised and inspired me. I began to have compassion for others labelled abusers too. I saw how I had needed to begin to see myself differently. This was similar to how I viewed those 'others' in society. I needed to develop more compassion and empathy for all of us.

This new perspective became my rally cry for anyone and everyone who was deemed throwaway by our society. These were the oft-described disgusting and despicable persons, who perpetrated all methods of violation on others, but in particular the women, children and animals of our world. *Those* people, the ones we have no answers or solutions for. We all just want them to go away or worse, to be dammed to an eternal hell.

I don't have the answer and I don't know who does, but I believe that we, as a society, need to figure these people out. The crimes they commit are tearing apart at our collective hearts, lives and communities and our society in general is suffering greatly. My only resource with which to deal with their acts of unkindness and cruelty, is to practice compassion and forgiveness, otherwise I fear that I would simply become the things I abhor most. Simple, not easy, but do- able.

A Little Bit Of Hope

While I was pondering this new and radical idea, I also decided that it was time to address my health. I'd been feeling increasingly run-down by the endless demands of the lifestyle I had taken on. This, as well as my ongoing, numerous personal crises and ever increasing customer service dramas.

It was the summer of 2009, and I just happened to stumble across a book called *Adrenal Fatigue-The 21st Century Stress Syndrome*. What I got from this book, was not what I expected to get. I thought I was buying a typical 'how to get well book' like the ones with titles such as 'how to beat your allergies' or 'how to be gluten-free' or 'how to get off dairy' etc. It started out that way, but quickly morphed into something much bigger than just adrenal fatigue. It was a plan of action, through its abundant and varied in-depth questionnaires, developed to pinpoint one's lifestyle contributors, at the crux of the underlying condition, which ultimately was much more than just adrenal fatigue.

I was a little put off by all the questions and thought "when did the 'how to get better' chapter begin?!" I felt tired just contemplating all the work I was going to have to do to complete the page upon page of questions and exercises, but I did them anyway. I had nothing better to do and I was in such a terrible state, sufficiently desperate enough to keep pushing on.

Out of this book came a much needed shift of perspective-I *wasn't* being tortured by life or anyone in my life. Not Debbie, the ministry, the insurance companies, the conglomerates, and nor the animal abusers. In fact, I was the only one doing the torturing and primarily to myself. I'd determined that what Debbie chose to do with her life was her responsibility, and I'd begin to let that go.

In the revealing tally of all those questions, I saw clearly how I was really only responsible for myself, and that was a tall enough task of its own.

Some Help For *The Change Of Life*

More glimmers of light came once I'd begun using hormone-replacement cream. Prior to this, I'd been a staunch believer that such things were too cruel to be considered as options, during this time in a woman's life cycle. I'd written nasty letters to the offending corporations responsible for the production of all those horse-urine based HRT products. I had carried placards in protest, and in general, harassed my friends and family nearly to tears regarding anything I'd thought was a travesty originating from the ignorance of human intervention.

Back then, I was a walking, talking protest of sorts. I'd supported animal rights groups and the anti-vivisection people. I was all about the animals and their plight. I was already a conflicted person before my injury, but I had the capacity to deal with these contradictions of thought-energy through my use of tools for coping with stress.

Meditation calmed my busy mind of its endless tirades, acting like a mood- levelling thermostat creating balance within my internal environment. Without this calming force, I was lost to my minds incessant ruminations and ramblings both inward and outward.

I'd always *talked* to myself out loud ever since I was a little girl. Most kids do actually, and it's only as we age, that this behaviour is then frowned upon. My dad talked out loud constantly, and as a child I'd enjoyed listening in. It was kind of an act of voyeurism, as there was seldom any other way or opportunity to get to know him or be a part of his world. His persistent, unchecked alcoholism prevented any chance of healthy familial interaction, and contributed hugely to the improbability of sibling harmony. As children, my siblings and I had a connection to one another similar to that of survivors of a catastrophe. We were bound by the formative event of often, what were the violent and unhealthy living conditions of our collective childhood.

More Light And A *Little* More Darkness Too.

Within a few months, of adding new and different combinations of bio-identical hormones to my living regimen, I was sleeping better, not great, but definitely better. Under the continued care of a gynecologist, my sleep and overall moods improved steadily over time. Hope continued to return ever so cautiously into my being.

A good example of my emerging state of mind then, happened one day when while on a short day-trip away from home. I had the opportunity to ponder and contemplate to myself, during the quiet and meditative time that driving in the countryside brings, when I suddenly had a major thought. *If I could love and accept the ugliest, darkest most difficult parts of me then, I could love and accept those same things in anyone and any situation.* It was a revelation, one that I could really build upon and, a very good place to start.

By the following year I was better, a lot better in fact and was more and more willing to let go of those embittered wars started the year previous.

It was another year, and the house remained un-sold. A new round of cleaning and constant de-cluttering and paring down had begun again.

I also come to a place emotionally where I could make some amends to Debbie. I apologised for my critical and mean nature of the past several years and went to great lengths to remind her that she hadn't deserved to be treated so poorly. I was ready to take responsibility for my behaviours and that truthfully, I just didn't have the coping tools for such an extreme living environment, one I'd only just barely survived.

In the spring of 2010, during a routine pap and physical examination, the doctor saw something that gave her a visible start. She verbally noted that something on my uterus did not look good. In fact, she muttered something such as, "it looks like cancer, or something like that". When you hear a comment like that, while your legs are still up in the stirrups, your vulnerability factor peaking, and there is literally nowhere to hide, it's a very harsh feeling indeed!

After months of waitlists, then a biopsy, it was determined that the offensive growth would be best left alone. It was good wake-up call and I'd reckoned not to allow myself to continue to live as I had been, in that mental place filled with gloomy thoughts and relentless self-pity. I had to keep up with the self-change, or I would probably die from some fall-out of disease and illness from the build-up of years from my lousy self-destructive attitudes.

No sooner had I got past the cancer scare, when a few weeks later, I experienced my first of several migraine *auras*. Up until then, my own experience of the phenomenon of migraine auras was like a vague idea, somewhere out there where other people suffered from them but not in here, not in my life.

All life, as you know it, stops when one has a good scare. There is nothing quite like it, except perhaps when we are confronted with the death of loved one.

One of my older brothers had been killed in a bizarre accident some years before, and my prevailing sense at the time was one of *waiting for something to happen.* Without consciously choosing to, I stopped thinking about everything, mind projections and all other planning, just to sit in that quiet space where time seemed frozen. Like his death and subsequent funeral, was the precursor to something else, the bigger event perhaps? It took some time for that sensation to pass.

Now, I was back in that space of time standing still, just as I had been a few weeks before, while waiting for the biopsy results.

After another round of tests, where the doctors determined that while my heart was strong, and appeared to be healthy, my overall state of health was lacking. I needed to take better care of myself immediately, or I would become something termed a *cardiac risk.* Somehow my cholesterol was through the roof despite some very good nutritional habits. I was being more honest with myself, more than I had been willing to be of late, and took out the magnifying glass to inspect my own life more closely.

The after-effects of the migraine aura hit me like a freight train. It had left me flat out drained and crippled with exhaustion for nearly four months. It was explained to me that I had experienced something like a mini-explosion in my brain. It couldn't have been worse timing, as winter was coming and so too the plowing and wood season with it. I would somehow have to tough it out for another winter, "the last one!" I assured myself.

But no amount of willpower was going to trump all the old and familiar brain injury symptoms brought on by the recent migraine episode. Talking, yet again, became a gargantuan effort and my head throbbed constantly. It was utterly devastating, to be back in that all-consuming place of crushing disability, once more.

I knew I couldn't face another winter without more help. Debbie had been gradually taking on more and more duties, and seemed extra willing to face her own life attitudes and shortcomings too. I called my good friend Sheila for help and within a few weeks, she had moved into the spare bedroom with her two dogs. Debbie saw this as an opportunity to go away for an extended visit with her family, which in turn gave me the time to sort out, un-harassed, all those lingering inconsolable hard feelings I harbored about our mutual predicament.

Time For A New Direction

I decided it was time to stop feeding my mind with constant thoughts of self-pity, regarding what was more realistically a budgetary issue with the ministry, and not a global conspiracy as I had been telling myself. After a short bout with nervousness, I made an appointment with a counsellor, one I'd have to pay for out my own pocket.

We only had one session, but that was enough to totally dislodge my world out of its relative complacency. I now had a plan of action and got myself readied to unveil it. I braced myself for the inevitable warfare that would predictably follow in its footsteps.

PART III

A SEPARATE REALITY

CHAPTER I-Changing
(JUST ABOUT) *EVERYTHING*

January-September 2011

"...most people do not like change, change is forced upon them by crisis and discontinuity. Thrown up against things, or into new arenas, we confront new possibilities and discover bits of ourselves we never knew were there. Discontinuity is a great learning experience but only if we survive it." From: The Age of Unreason by Charles Handy.

Gratefully, my friend, Sheila, was a witness to the insanity of my household on more than just one occasion. Through her help and her compassionate nature, I endeavored to understand what exactly I had been trying to deal with, in terms of what I deemed to be Debbie's many confounding behaviours.

Once Debbie returned from her time away, I instructed Sheila to go home. I was eternally grateful to her for all her help, both with the many chores and as an empathetic friend, but the time had come to address the many long-standing conflicts of interest in my relationship of plutonic co-habitants, with Debbie.

The counsellor had pointed out to me how irrational my current justification of continuing to give spousal-like support of Debbie's' lifestyle was, and that my rationalizations, quite seriously, undermined my own mental and emotional and physical stability.

I immediately cut off the supply of unlimited resources with which she had been using like a private health-care fund.

Looking back, it seems obvious that I should have done it long before then, but I didn't have the clarity of thought, under the fog of the several subsequent brain injuries, plus, I was much too absorbed in self-pity and guilt. I had relinquished the budget responsibilities to her, after months of harassment and personal attacks against my own spending impulses, but now I wanted it back. It had been 18 months since I'd seen a single document describing the state of our joint-finances. The kind that I'd generated, before giving in, out of guilt and exhaustion, to her demands.

Naturally she took these changes very badly as it was going to mean huge upheaval for both of us but mostly for her. It was a tricky time as we both adjusted to the new fiscal realities.

The Loss Of My Dad

I had just been treated to a lovely holiday trip to Chicago, to celebrate my upcoming 50th birthday, compliments of my dear friends Sheila, and her long-time partner. No sooner had I returned home, when the news came that my dad was ill and in hospital. I repacked and made the trip to Alberta where he lived with his second wife.

As sad as the moment was, sitting across from this gravely ill man I'd barely gotten to know, it was strangely comforting too. He would always be my dad and I was a lot like him. I had reconciled my own alcoholism nearly 20 years ago and had recommitted myself to addressing my raging tendencies. I only wished that he could have somehow confronted his own demons which had, for the better part of his life, successfully managed to deny himself and his loved ones of any semblance of familial intimacy.

He passed on a few days after I'd returned home.

More Trauma Around The Corner

With the financial separation well underway, my emotional and mental perspectives would soon follow. I finally came to the realization that I could not continue to rescue people unless, I'd reasoned, I started with myself first.

My rescuing tendencies had got me in some terrible binds

over the years. I had tried to help out a few friends by allowing them to stay in my little home for what amounted to subsidized living arrangements. However, the outcome was always the same. Total disaster! The subsequent damages and distress to the neighbors were both disheartening and embarrassing to me, so I put a plan together to move back in as soon as the necessary repairs were done.

I readied my little home for occupancy, enjoying being back in it and in the picturesque surroundings of my old neighborhood. It was so peaceful, and took me back to the simplicity of the life I once had there, and could presumably have again. But another trauma derailed my hopes of long-term serenity, and I had to make the heart wrenching decision to sell my little home.

On the one hand, it was another blow to the momentum of moving forwards, but on the other hand, I chose instead, to see it as an opportunity to relieve myself of a financial and emotional burden. As long as I had it to fall back on, I couldn't seem to address my immediate problems, as it had kept me in a permanent state of reminisce.

The recent trauma involved the unexpected death of one of our neighbors, whom Debbie had discovered within minutes of his passing. Her efforts to revive him fell short though, and she soon settled into the physical state of shock and the emotional state of inconsolable guilt. He had taken his own life soon after his marriage had collapsed, and we had been helping him out in the caring of his animals. When Debbie arrived to feed the dog, at his earlier request, we later surmised, that he had wanted one of us to find him that day.

For the first time in many years, I became an authentic friend to Debbie. This period of mourning lasted for months, and actually precipitated a peaceful-like energy over our lives.

I could think a little clearer now, and I nearly completely, but not quite, stopped all the yelling and demanding behaviours. I had written a little reminder note to myself during this time of relative mutual peace. In my efforts to stop the old habit of raising my voice whenever I felt threatened, I would read this note to myself.

"Go inside & find the part of myself that wants to";

- Move-on
- Travel
- Succeed
- Sell this House
- Heal my health and spiritual issues
- Eat well
- Connect & reconnect with others

"Then just sit with it. Reside there and trust. That's the part that needs to be heard. Not the negativity and fear."

"You don't have to raise your voice or yell to get your needs met. Remain calm so that others can hear you and respond. This will lower your agitation levels as well."

Over time, it worked wonders on the most resistant parts of my wounded self. I also realized that I'd have to do more forgiving of perceived hurts, if I wanted to continue to get better.

Some Very Bad News

I thought maybe I could get some rest then, but one more trauma was about to unfold with slow deliberate precision as Debbie's family was confronted with a difficult personal crisis. This meant that she would be away a lot, and I would be managing the home on my own for the most part.

This new trauma however, would prove to be so emotionally fracturing for her, that it would precipitate a dramatic shift of mutual circumstances.

CHAPTER II-More challenges
BUT A (FEW) MORE JOYS

October 2011-February 2012

"Time Heals. You will find over time, that the more you strive to become conscious of what has happened to you, the less you will be negatively affected by triggers and symptoms that used to cause you distress. Known triggers and symptoms will be less debilitating and hidden ones will become less transparent and easier to live with." From: Objects in the Mirror are Closer than they Appear

It was inconceivable to me then, that I'd have to consider the possibility of spending another winter in that house, with Debbie. I wouldn't allow myself to go there unless absolutely necessary. Yes, I'd done my share of emotional and mental repairing of hurts and traumas, but this was enough already, surely *good-timing* was on my side?!

But, before that question could be answered, I experienced another migraine aura episode. It happened one afternoon when I was driving home from running some errands, and rounded the big bend in the road, the one I had nearly driven off of out of despair two years previous. It was then I noticed a dark plume of black smoke rising high above into the perfect blue sky but no-less, rising above what I was convinced was my house!

I could not drive fast enough, as visions of burning cats, dog and bird filled my consciousness, and I became fully panic-stricken. Not until I drove into the driveway of my home, could I then feel certain that things were in fact okay, and only then was I able to consciously take a breath. I got out of my car and had stood next to it resting my body up against the driver's door breathing heavily, and trying to make some sense of what I just witnessed. I'd ponder to myself whether I had been hallucinating and was I crazy?!

I stood for a moment and then heard the unmistakable sounds of the burning and crackling of an advancing fire. Then I saw it. It was across the road from my house, burning and spreading up the hillside above, and below, towards my home, a house that was once described as being "wrapped in kindling" by its previous owners.

I made all the necessary phone calls, and inquired with my neighbors and determined that it was unintentionally set. Soon, the firemen with their trucks filled with water made quick work of extinguishing the menacing flames from advancing further. It had been a very close call for all of us. I later heard from one of my neighbors, that someone living in a rented trailer had inadvertently started the fire that nearly destroyed all of our properties, and who knows what else. (I'd actually driven up to that trailer to check up on the occupants, when a man, who I obviously startled and disturbed from a deep slumber, came running out in panic towards the car!). The fire chief stated that he'd estimated we all had less than five more minutes, before the flames would have developed into an all-out forest fire situation. This was a commonly known fact of life, which, as rural property dwellers is tantamount to that of total property and lifestyle loss.

Within moments of finally sitting down to absorb it all, the migraine came on without warning. It had begun with a tingling feeling over most of the left side of my body spreading eventually to my face and head, and simultaneously, my field of vision narrowed to a long tunnel with an extreme bright light at the end of it. My auditory senses interpreted all sounds as though echoed. As I gradually came out of these altered sensory states, squiggly lines would then appear to the left and right peripheries of my field of vision. Ironically, the persistent headache so often associated with migraines, wouldn't materialize for several more days then would remain, unabated, for three or four weeks afterwards.

But it was the debilitating fatigue that would soon come, which was the worst part of all.

A month later, we came to the painful realization that it was time to let go of our dog, the 'special case'. She was only 5, but had the health issues of a dog three times her age, and nothing could make up for the earlier life traumas she had endured before coming into our lives. For the first time, she had been permitted to be a dog, not a showpiece, and not a puppy-factory or some ill-conceived behavioural modification experiment, as one of her prior owners had insisted was possible.

I made my own peace with her before that day came, recognising that I had contributed some added grief, but at times, had co-existed in her life with all the good stuff too.

Opportunity For A Break

Within weeks of my dogs passing, I got a phone call from my old friend, Larry. He had since moved away, back to the big city, and was now planning a trip abroad. He wanted me to join him in his adventure to East Asia and, I would need to be ready to go in 5 days! At first I seriously considered the prospect of a trip, after all I thought, I could really use a break.

The reality, however, was that I'd be just too tired to even feel excited about it. These were the thoughts of a radically different Michelle, not the one who on average travelled to foreign lands at least twice per year, played team sports in all four seasons, and just in general led an exciting life! That was the old Michelle and the old life, where I was a working person earning a decent wage and enjoying all the benefits of good health. She would have been thrilled at the prospect of such exotic travel opportunity!

It was too just much to contemplate then, so I had to quickly decline the offer.

Life is so strange sometimes, because a few days on, my

friend Sheila called to invite me on a trip to Costa Rica, leaving in January, in about 2 months' time. "Okay", I thought, I should be feeling a lot better by then?

With Debbie's personal life difficulties demanding more and more of her time and energy, this translated into us spending less and less time around one another, which was a very good thing. We had fewer opportunities to get on each other's nerves, thus generating a lot less conflict too.

I had saved a few dollars from the sale of my little house and even though the prudent thing would have been to sock it away and use it for a fresh start at some future time, I reasoned then, that I desperately needed a break first.

Debbie was away for the better part of that winter and the following spring. Her absence made it probable for me to take on all the responsibilities of yet another winter season at the big house.

The rejections of prospective buyers became increasingly difficult to not take personally. As crazy as that may seem the process of trying to sell one's home, in a plummeting market, can be so draining and so demoralizing that you just want it to end, and reach the point where you don't care how that happens.

I had already reached that point.

While Debbie was away, I had taken the time to get to know some of my neighbors a bit more. They were an interesting cross-section of people, and a few characters too. I was saddened about having to eventually leave them all behind.

It was easier to prepare for my upcoming trip to Costa Rica in the quiet solitude of my home, and the pets were much calmer too. The cats were no longer fighting with one another, now that the dog and Debbie, along with the massive amounts of anxiety they collectively generated, were absent from the house as well.

I Think I'm Going To Die?!

Before I got on the plane, I'd been prescribed all the relevant pills and vaccines for a trip to a country in the tropics. The plan was to take the malarial meds one week prior, then once per week after that for the duration of the trip. That sounded simple enough, so I'd taken the first anti-malarial dose eight days prior to leaving, but within about ten hours of taking it, I knew something wasn't quite right with me.

Many people after acquiring a brain injury develop sensitivities with medications, even those that they've taken prior to becoming injured, including some of the over-the-counter variety. I was one of those *sensitive* people.

When I was still drinking alcoholically, I didn't think to read the fine print, "who does that anyway?" I'd think to myself. Whenever taking some medications like those for allergies, cough and cold etc. I *never* even considered it, especially since my prevailing mindset then, was that I knew better than pretty much anybody. Arrogance and self-righteousness (fear-disguised as self-confidence) got me through life or so I convinced myself at the time.

As a brain injured person, I often just simply forgot to read the insert, the one that is there for a reason. This time however I *was* careful to read the fine print given all the horror stories I'd heard and read about anti-malaria drugs. I recall reading nothing in the package insert to even hint at the possibility of an unpleasant side-effect. I checked-in with my medical professional-type friends and felt assured, enough so that about 10pm Friday night, I popped that pill into my mouth, and never gave it a second thought. That was until, things started to go sideways.

After 10 hours, I thought this is not a big deal and I could totally handle this. It was a piece of cake. Then, no sooner had I thought that, when I began to feel ever so slightly- off, similar to when one of those migraine auras comes on. But by about noon that day I was certain that I was dying, not sooner or later but, that I was actually in the throes of dying.

Persistent hallucinations and conversations with others, even though I was alone, continued on for unknown hours. The vomiting started around 8pm later that same day and lasted until the following Monday afternoon, nearly 2 days later. I retched and retched long after there was even a speck of food left in my system and I'm pretty sure that the cats and bird did not get fed or watered during the bulk of that time. I don't recollect much during those few days. I didn't possess the capacity to think through what was happening to me. I hadn't been able to formulate a clear thought, so it had never occurred to me to call anyone, much less 911.

It took several more days to feel secure enough in the belief that the worst was truly over. Except by then, it was just a few short days before I was to get on a plane, several in fact, and travel for nearly 20 plus hours, across 3 time zones and countless climactic regions. I determined during the haze of sickness, that it was improbable I was going to make that flight or get to enjoy my dream vacation. The necessary break I'd been obsessing about for years was not going to happen, and I became inconsolable.

Somehow though, I got myself together and along with the sympathetic assistance of my travel companions, I made that flight after all. Once airborne, nothing mattered and I rationalized that I could rest, once settled in at our final destination.

That trip completely rejuvenated my spirit, but did nothing to alter the tenacious and ever-present fatigue. Still, it was an important step in the ongoing progression of reclaiming me as a whole person, through the continuous, steady goal-driven work towards stabilizing my emotional and mental as well as physical and spiritual health.

Another shift of sorts had occurred within my psyche, and I suddenly became more open to hearing and reading about things that I hadn't been able to take in, prior to that time. I suddenly became more available to what I always believed was a divine creative energy. I became aware, surprisingly so, of a tentative reconnection to My Source.

PART IV

THE END IS BUT A BEGINNING

CHAPTER I-ANGELS KNOCKING AT MY (FRONT) DOOR

March -May 2012

"Prayers are not successfully made unless there is rapport between the conscious and subconscious mind of the operator (the one doing the praying). This is done through imagination and faith" from: Prayer: the Art of Believing by Neville Goddard.

The local library used-book sell-off events became my new source for good books, and this subsequently bought all manner of good and useful ideas, which started flowing through me and into my life. I'd be flooded with exciting new concepts and ideals with which to spend my time in contemplation of. It was good timing because the after-effects of the last migraine lingered on well into the spring of 2012. Thus, solitary and low-key activities were very agreeable co-habits during this time.

I rediscovered prayer and tried once again to sit in meditation but with pitiful results. I couldn't yet get a handle on the stream of consciousness manifesting as incessant self-chatter, which was basically impossible to ignore.

I read and read. Gratefully my vision and brain health had returned sufficiently enough to allow me some enjoyment from this long lost passion (the ten year anniversary of the accident was just around the corner). Fatigue made the task more challenging, but my determination was so strong then, that nothing could have prevented me from at least trying to absorb some quality written material each and every day.

I Can Do It! What's That?

My older sister and I chatted on the phone one day when she mentioned, off-hand, how bummed out she was that her hero, mentor *and* saviour was coming to speak at a conference in Vancouver, and she, my sister, was broke, so she couldn't go. I sympathized as good sisters do, and as she continued to talk about it I kind of drifted off a bit (my ability to focus remained an elusive skill then) when I heard several names I immediately recognised-Marianne Williamson (*my* personal hero & saviour!), Louise Hay and Wayne Dyer (my mentors).

I then became absolutely freaked out myself, at the prospect of seeing these giants of the self-help movement. In my mind, they were nothing short of spiritual-quest Gurus. In that moment, I reckoned to find a way to get us both to that conference.

In keeping with the teachings of Neville Goddard, 'Living from the End,' I had practiced and practiced his methods of bringing about my chosen reality, which was to go to the conference, as though this desire had already materialized itself into my life. An income tax refund, was the final piece to the puzzle, and soon we'd both be on our way to Vancouver to meet our heroes (and saviours!).

Glimpses Of A (Possible) Future

There had been two other occasions in my life where I consulted tarot card interpreters. I determined not to put huge amounts of energy into these readings, but instead used the insights exposed within the reading like a compass bearing. They would point the way and the direction, but I'd still have to make all the relevant life choices, and take the appropriate actions in order to bring about the potential outcomes.

I was still kind of new to the little town where I relocated to five years ago, and needed some help finding the right tarot person, so I consulted someone I'd connected with through shared personal hardships, and she gave me a name. Within a few days I got my reading, and it had really blown my mind. It revealed to me the kind of information that can really generate a lot of energy and motivation in a person's life. Such was the reading I got then.

My sister and I rendezvoused in the big city for the experience of a lifetime and I got exactly what I needed, and much, much more. Meeting and speaking with Marianne Williamson will definitely rank near the top as the highlight of my entire life.

The Painful Endings Of Several Journeys

A week before to leaving for my pilgrimage, my relationship with Debbie had taken a dramatic downwards turn. It happened immediately after she got some tough news regarding the continued poor health of one of her parents.

My friend, Sheila, had stayed behind to care for my pets, while I was away. This was much to the dismay of Debbie, after going through a very agonizing loss in her personal life, the day before I was to leave.

Naturally she was grief-stricken and angry, and I'd have been a good punching bag but I wasn't going to take it on. I knew already that the prospects of a continued relationship, of any kind, were not in either of our best interests. By then, the open wounds of too much hurt, betrayal and emotional scarring, had made healing the friendship, impossible. I sympathized with her silently, as we weren't on very good speaking terms by then, nor did she accept any of my attempts to console her. It was very painful at the time to see her in that state of brokenness and despair, and not be able to help in any way.

I knew then that the relationship had run its course, and we were at the crossroads, each taking our separate roads.

Before I returned home after the conference, I managed to convince another friend to escort me on the return trip. I'd been feeling a sense of foreboding for a few days, and my suspicions were fueled further by the many frequent, disturbing phone calls from Sheila, regarding Debbie's aggressive and indifferent state of mind, and her distressing physical appearance as well. I just felt too afraid to go home alone.

The day before I was to return home, Sheila called, sounding quite frantic, telling me that Debbie was missing. She hadn't come home from the previous day's outing. The idea of suicide crossed my mind ever so fleetingly. I called her family and sure enough she was with them. She had left without a word to anyone leaving her pets in limbo. Gratefully though, Sheila had taken care of all the animals in my absence, including her own two large dogs.

I felt a huge relief inside knowing, I'd be alone at home, after Sheila went back to her own life, a little worse for wear.

Another Shift And Another Twist

Irony was about to make yet another appearance in my life.

The following morning, as I was sitting on the sofa contemplating all the things which had transpired that year, especially the changes I'd experienced and all the internal shifts, I came to a place where I made a decision.

I realized that I'd been on a kind of *healing plateau* for several years by then, and I often noted to myself in the course of my brain injury recovery that periods of repair seemed to alternate with periods of stasis, where nothing seemed to change. I'd get to a point of growth then stop, sometimes for a year or more, then suddenly becoming aware of more expansion in my thinking and remembering abilities. Recovery can be so subtle, that sometimes it's as if nothing is happening, but what I've now recognised as stasis, is actually similar to a scheduled *down time* for maintenance and repairs.

As I'd been contemplating all this stuff, I came to the conclusion that, because I'd been so stuck, I hadn't been able make good decisions for myself for some time. I'd been trapped in the galvanised thinking of someone who would not or could not accept alternative outcomes to their problems.

My friends and a few family members had been telling me

for years to get out of the current predicament, but I developed many good reasons as to why I had to stay. My contempt for what I perceived as ignorance and over-simplification of my complex set of troubles conspired to smother my world in the very same ignorance. I suppose if someone *had* come up with an alternative idea, perhaps I could have possibly run with it, but more often I only heard the desperate pleadings from those loved ones who felt utterly helpless. They were unable to offer any other alternatives, and they simply couldn't find any other way to help me, but to plead.

Eventually I was able to listen. My good friend Sheila, bless her, had been making some useful suggestions about how I could move on from the present chaos.

At last the day had arrived where I'd became sufficiently teachable to *get it*, what some people had been telling me, and in some cases yelling at me, all along. I'd had other choices available to me all along. The primary issue was a pattern of reluctance to make a move. Strange, and ironic, when you consider my life's historical habit which was to pack up and run every one to two years!

Why then had I become so hesitant to move on when my environment was so hostile?! Because I'd somehow convinced myself that I couldn't abandon Debbie. She had put most of her life-savings into the house, and I felt at least partially responsible for the decision to buy it, so this fact weighed heavily on my conscience. I already had one bankruptcy, and I didn't relish the thought of coming back from a second one.

What it boiled down to was this. Yes, she had invested her savings, but I had invested nearly every penny of my income, every ounce of my energy and literally my blood, sweat and tears into the house and, also into caring for her when she could not or would not care for herself or her pets.

Also the loss and irreparable damage to my mental, emotional and spiritual self were completely at stake, if I had chosen to remain there any longer.

The time had come, and one of us absolutely *had* to go.

Before this new sense of direction could mould itself into something concrete like a plan of action, there came a knock at my door, snapping my attention back into the present moment. At first I didn't recognize these people, but they did look a little familiar to me. It was a few of Debbie's family members, sans Debbie.

What happened next was nothing short of miraculous! Within 20 minutes, we had a signed agreement, and then the following morning another offer surfaced which I would not refuse. I was going to permanently leave and relinquish all responsibilities for the home and property. The only caveat was that my name was to remain on the mortgage, not ideal but perfectly fantastic!

I was leaving, and only had two weeks to pack up and move out. In the fog of bliss, I somehow figured I would only need two weeks to untangle years of entanglement, but I did it, with legions of help in the process.

Before leaving, I held a 'burning of documents' party and with some assistance, purged nearly eleven boxes representing 17 years of insurance claims and litigation. It was high time I figured, to move on from the victim identity I had been unconsciously nurturing and hanging on to.

I kept only a few relevant medical documents for the purpose of reference in the writing of this book, the remainder provided a beautiful blazing inferno for nearly 6 hours!

CHAPTER II-THE ADVENTURE THAT NEVER WAS

June - July 2012

'Self and Self-image'
"It is vitally important to understand the relationship between your 'self' and your 'self-image' before you start on a vision quest so that you don't waste your energy looking for the wrong thing. You will never find your self-image without finding yourself first, because self-image is a reflection of the self." From Objects in the Mirror are Closer than they Appear

The previous year, just before the second migraine episode happened, I had bought a well-used travel trailer. The idea at the time was that at some future point, I was going to embark on an epic cross-country family pilgrimage of sorts. Using money from the last of my savings, I purchased an old truck, so that I could tow my trailer, and relocate to as yet unknown greener pastures. Before any travels could be undertaken, it was to first become my home, but where to park it?

My dear neighbor, hearing of my predicament graciously invited me, my trailer along with my pets, (who were in complete shock and dismay of this apparent next chapter in their lives!) to camp-out in her yard for as long as was necessary.

The Improbable Adventure

My latest plan was to visit some family in various towns in the province, all the while living in the trailer with my two elderly cats. This, I rationalized was completely doable, but the fact that I'd never towed trailer before was a constant source of anxiety, which was best not overly indulged.

After only a few weeks of preparations, I waved goodbye to my neighbor then set out on my pilgrimage. I got less than 100 kilometers into my journey, when a host of mechanical problems permanently derailed my plans. Another wrench, and in no time I became unglued. I just didn't have the emotional room for deviations from my plan of action.

I felt then, that I absolutely had to keep a promise to my sister to help her move out of a bad situation and into a better one. I was unknowingly attempting to somehow relive and repeat my last set of life circumstances. Change, I reckoned, is often not as easy as it pretends to be.

Getting sucked into more rescuing, was just an old habit. No one was asking, yet I was still offering up myself, as though I had some secret superpower which gave me access to infinite amounts energy and unlimited resources to rescue others. *Not this time!* Came the response from the universe.

A good friend bailed me out with her credit card, so that I could get the truck repaired sufficiently enough to continue, but not on the trip I originally planned for. I had to deviate to the nearest town for repairs, and while I waited in my little trailer, with my stressed out cats in 35C heat, my situation became painfully obvious to me. I needed to scrap my plan entirely.

I remembered passing an RV campsite on the way into town, my truck limping past, with acrid smoke billowing out of the rear tires as the brake drums fused to the rotors, and all the while, the thermostat needle tipped into the red zone. I could always just pull in there and call it a day I thought. It was an option.

By six pm, the repairs were completed and I was free to carry on. I'd started out on this day full of hope and excitement in anticipation of my great adventure, but that seemed like a lifetime ago now.

I hooked up the trailer once again, and headed north towards some friends who lived about a 3 hour drive away. I decided to try and get that far at least before figuring out what to do next.

I'd just passed through the next town, a mere 30 minutes into the restart of my journey, when my truck overheated. I pulled off the busy highway onto a narrow shoulder, put the truck in park, then put my head in my hands and began to cry. I managed to get myself organised enough to make a tear-filled plea to the repair garage, but they had since closed for the day and their answering service could offer absolutely no assistance whatsoever.

After hanging up from what was a dead end, I returned my head to my hands feeling a familiar, hollowed-out sensation. I think I was in shock.

I don't remember how long I was parked and sitting in that state, but at some point someone yelled over the constant roar of traffic towards me "are you OK?!"

"NO, I'm not OK!" I yelled back to the tow truck operator, whose massive truck was at a complete stop in the fast lane, across from the two lanes next to me, facing the opposite direction of my vehicle!

His girlfriend, seated next to him recognised me as they were driving past. She was from that small town I moved to 5 years previously, and had commanded him to stop and try to help, and so he did! Things got sorted out sufficiently to the point where I could just get myself and, by now, hyper-stressed cats and convoy of rattletrap truck & trailer back down to the RV site I'd passed by earlier that day.

Ordinarily a breakdown wasn't the end of the world, not even a series of breakdowns, but, I wasn't in an 'ordinary state' of being, yet. All the difficulties of the previous year's still shadowed my psyche. Trying to navigate life with a brain injury means bare minimum rest and I hadn't yet rested sufficiently enough to recharge myself, and in so doing, inject my life with the necessary energy and self-belief to meet with life on life's terms. I remained too ragged inside to be able to confront life's many, sometimes recurrent, challenges.

Getting Some Rest & Regrouping

Towing a nearly twenty year old-22 foot trailer with an unreliable vehicle may not sound like any ones idea of a holiday, but it became a holiday of sorts for me. Once I got my trailer backed into the designated space at the RV campsite, with a great deal of patient coaching by the camp attendant, I actually felt for the first time in 5 years, free, again.

The feelings then, were similar to those that I experienced just after having arrived in that small town from the big city, to start what I'd imagined was a better life, a life of my choosing.

After struggling with the trailer's awning for more than hour, and about ready to pack it in, some neighbors came to my rescue and kindly sorted it all out for me. I hooked up the water, sewer, power then finally the satellite dish. I felt pretty pleased with myself, until I just couldn't seem to get the dish oriented properly enough to get a good signal. Exhausted, I climbed back in to my little trailer, my sanctuary and collapsed on the bed. I tried to rest, but couldn't so I gave the satellite dish one more try before officially giving up. About an hour later and only after the rains come, soaking me through every layer of clothing, did I finally manage to get a satellite-signal and it was just strong enough. Now, I determined I could get some rest.

I stayed in that beautiful campsite for 5 days, my good friend's credit card coming in handy once again.

The site I'd been assigned overlooked a small creek, which was busy with all the various activities of birds and water critters going about their daily living regimes. On the water's surface were isolated islands of pink and white water lilies, looking reminiscent of lotus flowers. I would lie on my bed for hours looking out of the tiny window, lost in all the beauty laid out before me.

It was the perfect spot to be, in that moment in time, as it provided an atmosphere of peacefulness with which to reflect upon this specific phase of my new life's journey.

Soon I would be on the move again.

After another repair job, thankfully minor in nature, but not cheap however, I was at last able to get under way with renewed confidence in myself and my truck. I made it to a predetermined campground location a few miles out of range of the city where my good friends lived. There I stayed for a full ten days, getting proper rest, and just enjoying nature and the company of close friends.

I hadn't realize that my little camp-spot was perched above a busy train track, but after several occasions of being startled awake in the middle of the night, I eventually got semi-used to the noises and repetitive predicable sounds made by the trains as they passed by. My cats on the other hand, were not at all impressed with all the seemingly endless disturbances and upsets to their tenuous states of serenity.

In the relative peace and quiet of the campground, I'd been able to do some good thinking and formulated another plan of action. It was obvious that I could not afford the gypsy lifestyle, no matter how hard I believed it was my birthright.

My father, before he'd passed away told me that his dream-life would be to live as a gypsy, not having to deal with the responsibilities of caring for a house or yard and not being tied down to employment, but rather to work when necessary, not as vocation. I suddenly understood then, my own inner yearnings to continually be on the move and not tied to anyone or anything, a free spirit. I romanced myself with this idea ever since hearing my fathers' words.

It was time leave my little campsite oasis.

I had endeared myself to my neighbors sufficiently enough that they would welcome me back, trailer-in-tow for as long as was needed. I packed up and headed back to my little town, not ever thinking that I'd be going back to that place of hardship so soon after what felt like an illusionist's escape maneuver just to leave in first place.

One very promising possibility came out of my unscheduled visit to the friend's town, near to where I'd been camped for those 10 days. I had been given a walkthrough of their rental suite and loved what I saw. It would be ready for occupancy, possibly as soon as August 1. I made an immediate commitment to take it. The impending re-location would prove to be the most grueling and difficult move of mine, ever.

CHAPTER III-TRAILER LIFE

July & August 2012

"Rather than think you need to go on an archaeological dig in your personal history, just look at your life in the present moment to see what your past beliefs have created." From Women's bodies, Women's wisdom, by Christiane Northrup MD

It was with conflicted feelings that I retraced my steps back to the place where so much difficulty and bad feelings remained.

I parked my trailer in a beautiful spot next to several blooming lilac trees. Living in my neighbor's front yard was akin to living in a park. She'd spent many hours patiently planting and parenting the abundant varieties of roses, lilies, lilacs and other fantastically fragrant blossoming plants, most of which I'd never heard of. There was a small robust creek ambling through the many trees and tall grasses on its way down through the rolling hills where the property was nestled. It was quiet and serene. It was the perfect place for me.

Not too far down the road were all the reminders of my previous existence. My house, the property, all the wildlife and my other neighbor whose lone horse, Mandy, had endeared herself to me. I was still too raw to even consider driving in that direction, so I just stayed clear of it altogether.

As I settled in, no matter how hard I tried to convince myself otherwise, I could not escape the feeling that I was in danger. I felt a deep sense of foreboding, much like when I'd gone to the conference in the previous month, and needed a friend to escort me home. I just couldn't shake it. If you've ever felt this way, you'll relate to what I'm describing here. It's not a feeling associated with any particular thought, rather it's as if it exists all by itself. There's no context or back-story, just the unshakable and persistent feelings of dread.

It took some time, but eventually the sense of dread passed, and thus I could just enjoy my surroundings.

I determined then, that I better figure out the how and the why of my choices in life, or else I'd be doomed to repeat them. I honestly did not believe that I was going to survive my last relationship, and I became convinced that I wouldn't survive the next one, if it looked remotely close to the previous disaster I'd often termed as resembling 'an utter train-wreck'.

Once settled into the trailer life, meant that I could read some good books, but mostly, I'd sit in quiet contemplation of my current predicament. I restarted some nighttime meditation in the form of a soft music cd by Dr. Wayne Dyer, and I could at least fall asleep sooner while listening to the beautiful melodies, than was my typical pattern of restlessness and unconscious resistance.

Soon I began to take some stock of my life and its toxic and dysfunctional behavioural patterns. This could be another good beginning. After all the pain and all the battles and all the wars I'd initiated, via the collective fears of feeling abandoned, unwanted and unloved, all of that brought me to this place, living in a travel trailer, parked like a squatter in my neighbors front yard. This was nothing like what I'd hoped, much less imagined, for myself.

I'd be 51 years of age by the end of that week, and from my perspective, brain injury had stolen the previous ten years. Yes, I'd learned a ton, and ultimately had become a better person for it, more compassionate especially, but, those ten years were lost forever. They were the ones that were supposed to be the prime of my life.

This thought used to harass me constantly until I'd come up with a suitable rebuttal. As long as I could get on a surfboard and catch a wave, I'd retain my youthful exuberance. This idea, for me, became a *mission impossible* of a kind.

I re-dedicated myself to writing my long-forgotten book of my brain injury experience, which you're now reading. I felt confident about writing it, not because I considered myself a writer then, but I had been journaling on my computer for a while and had racked up 200 or so pages of ramblings...a good start I figured!

Most of my things were locked away in several storage lockers in town, and I always avoided having to go in there for anything other than something of extreme importance, because they were that big of a nightmare to navigate. I would have to just face it though, if I wanted to get this book underway, so I spent the next two weeks organising, holding several garage-sales and various other 'sell-off of possessions' schemes until I could actually get to the files and boxes I needed to retrieve my precious disk of book notes. I brought back several promising boxes and crates filled with disks and papers.

Nowhere, in any of that, were my notes. They were gone, vanished and I felt completely destroyed inside. With all the moving packing and unpacking and shuffling things here and there, they were just gone.

The painful truth was that I'd have to start over, from nothing. Another familiar pattern, it seemed, was revisiting my life-the pattern of starting over with nothing. Several more weeks passed before I could confront the blank document that was my book. I managed only a few pages, and then shut it all down for good. I wasn't able to write through the grief of loss of all those incredible insights, or so I'd convinced myself.

Thankfully though, I'd be moving soon, moving into my new home and another fresh start and maybe, just maybe I really could live differently. I would soon busy myself with all the details of moving and forget about the book entirely.

Having to plan and pull-off a cross-province move was probably more than I could realistically manage, but I was a one person act, if not me then who else was going to do it? My friends came out of the woodwork and donated their time and their efforts, some of them coming from hundreds of miles away! The move was nothing short of a mammoth combined effort, simply a brutal affair, but, we got it done. Just another convoy to yet another town, this *was* the business of moving Michelle!

CHAPTER IV-THE (ONGOING) REBIRTH OF INNER-BLISS

September 2012-Infinity & Beyond!!

'Reclaiming Your Life'
"The most important point to remember, as you recreate your life, is that you are the artist who is painting the picture of yourself for yourself in your mind, even though you think you are creating it to be seen through the eyes of others. In a sense your brain injury has given you the rare opportunity to consciously recreate yourself as you really are and not just as you think you want others to see you" from, Objects in the Mirror are closer than they Appear.

My definition of a YOGI; calm, confident, unassuming, kind, gentle, generous, humorous and light, empathetic, social, wise, complimentary-conscious of every moment.

This was retrieved from a note I'd made to myself the preceding year and now, I wanted to get to that place again. Only this time, I was bearing the gifts of wisdom and empathy. Those two essential levels of consciousness which had escaped me once I'd become too injured and could no longer grasp their subtleties.

As resolute as I was to recapture my Yogi-mind, reality soon settled into my weary bones, the fact was that I'd become totally exhausted and could do no more.

Getting Back To *Normal*
Months passed before I could unpack sufficiently to see beyond the towering stacks of boxes that had clogged every part of my tiny suite. Having my good friends so near to me

was a gift far beyond any I'd imagined. I'd been alone and isolated for so long that I didn't realize how incredibly insignificant as a person I'd become in my own mind. These people not only showered me with their love, but they included me in much of their lives as well, and I once again felt like I belonged somewhere, and in the hearts of someone, several someone's in fact.

During the preceding several months of moving, squatting then moving again, I'd rescheduled an important specialist appointment. It was critical that I get the low-down on those recurrent migraine episodes as I experienced yet another, mini-episode just after the move, so I could see a pattern of stress creating the pattern of migraine-auras, but how could I interrupt it? Was that even possible?

After arriving late to my appointment, (I'd written down the time incorrectly) then having to endure the next fifteen minutes being chastised for it, the doctor at last settled in to the business of my problem. To my relief he turned out to be a fantastic guy, and he helped me to get clearer in mind and also to create a plan of action for healthier living. This would surely beguile himself to me for time immemorial, how ironic I thought to myself then.

Sometimes, medical realities can be too bleak to be considered, such was mine so I preferred, instead, to act as if I was already well, and live in accordance with this precept and immediately put the new plan of action to work.

I immediately begin to first walk more, and then get back into other lost passions, like hiking and backpacking. I managed through proper diet and walking, to drop 20 pounds of accumulated despair in the shape of a spare tire wrapped around my waist!

The ruinous habit of hanging onto resentments was never going to get me anywhere. I'd have to face the unfathomable and start the act of forgiving everyone in my life who I thought had ever treated me poorly, and number one on that list was Debbie. Not a single day had passed where I wasn't reliving some past nasty conversation or nasty situation involving her. I had to somehow try to let it go and move on.

The Remnants Of Rage

Brain injury conspires to keep one stuck in self-righteous indignation much like alcoholism and addiction of all matters and descriptions. Holding onto justifiable anger is like hanging onto a grenade long after the pin has been pulled, sooner not later, it will hurt, maim or kill you! Either way no one gets out unscathed and my resentments were the equivalent of a hand-full of grenades.

My appearance had visibly aged by nearly ten years so I not only lost the ten years that I considered to be my prime years, but, I lost an additional 10 years to the ravages of resentment and other toxic beliefs, excessive physical labour and the toll one takes when caring for an unwell person. When I was still living in the big house with Debbie, I recalled watching a documentary where it was estimated that for every year a parent or caregiver takes care of a sick or mentally challenged child or other person, they lose 4 years off their lifespan. I was stunned when I heard that and this 'fact' enraged me then to the point, where it fed into the domino-effect of resentment, anger, rage and mental abusiveness.

I continue to come back from this experience, but have successfully turned it around in my mind, for the most part and I now see it as a necessary learning curve with several enormous U-turns thrown in. I needed to learn these things and Debbie facilitated my learning the many essential life lessons through the mutual adversity that was our relationship.

A 'Miracle'called Holosync

Within a week of seeing the Neurologist something amazing happened. I received an email that I was tempted to just delete but something caught my eye and my attention-'people with brain-injuries and other forms of head trauma report excellent results'. Ok, I thought, now my attention was fully engaged. I was broke at the time plus one of my cats had needed some intense vet-care but I was feeling so certain about this idea; that electronically generated alpha and theta brain wave patterns could be an answer for me-for my inability to meditate or sit peacefully without the ever-present, non-stop brain musings I was prone to. I sent away for it and spent the last of my income on a hunch, yet, and I don't know why exactly, but I'd felt extremely confident it could work for someone like me.

To my utter joy and relief, it did exactly as promised! I've been using this amazing technology as a path back to my bliss ever since.

One More U-Turn

My first Christmas in my new home would not be spent there after all. Another good friend of mine used some of her amassed air miles to send me on a little trip of a family get-together experience over the holidays.

I'd been feeling tremendous fear in the pit of my stomach for a few weeks after booking the flight. I tried to talk myself out of the feeling, but they persisted. I'd reasoned to myself that it was after all *my family,* and I never really felt that connected to most of my siblings or parents either.

I had become broken and vulnerable as a brain injured person, and I'd allowed myself to believe that they could somehow be present and show up. My family unit was terribly fractured, and no amount of wishful thinking was going to change that. Prior to my injury, I'd purposefully not had much contact with several family members, because they were so uncomfortable with me. They were uncomfortable with my sexual orientation, my admitted alcoholism and perhaps, what some may have viewed as weakness, such as my acceptance of having (some) needs.

My new self-had many more needs than my old self, and I really think this may have further destabilised the fragile unit that was my family. I was no longer independent or capable and more accurately was, for a time, unreliable. I didn't work and thus had no associated value or identity with which to compare one's self to. My comprehension and vocabulary, pitifully handicapped, made it uncomfortable for everyone when trying to converse.

Who I was now, I reckoned, took some of them too far beyond their comfort levels, so to cope with the new me, meant that they just felt sorry for me.

My visit, scheduled for 7 days lasted barely two. My Mom and I hit the wall of dysfunction soon after I arrived, but curiously something amazing came out of the ashes of that experience. I felt afterwards as though *something had been broken, so that something else could get fixed.* As difficult as it was, to leave her house feeling so rejected and punished, I quickly turned things around being open to the understanding of the bigger picture. I could love her exactly the way she was but that didn't mean I had to lay myself out there as a bulls-eye for her target practice. I could love and accept her from afar; she is after all The Warrior Queen! One day, I imagine, I will feel sufficiently strong enough to *not* take on the toxicity of my tribal inheritance.

AFTERWARD

The Journey Of Healing & Discovery That Never Ends...

"Most people never run far enough on their first wind to find out they've got a second. Give your dreams all you've got and you'll be amazed at the energy that comes out of you."
William James

&

"Take your dreams very, very seriously" Barbara Sher

Time heals most things. My brain for example, although still damaged, has healed to the point where I could seriously consider writing this book.

Many of the earlier physical difficulties did eventually heal or lessen somewhat. My vision problems became much less of an issue by about the fifth year post-accident. The bizarre sensory issues I experienced soon after the accident slowly returned to manageable symptomology, but I still, very occasionally, smell that old familiar rotting-garbage stench but generally only around a migraine event. My other senses remain dulled to this day but seem more tolerable to me. I really believe that once I started to re-establish a connection to my inner-self, the other problems seemed a lot less pressing, thus more manageable.

Until you re-connect with your new self, life will be scary and you will feel uncertain about most things, but just keep going because you will come back. Only this time, you'll be new & improved and maybe even funnier than you were before (at least to yourself anyway!). Above all else, do the work of getting well, because that's always going to be your responsibility.

Gratefully, my physical self continues to get well, and even though I continue to have constant, daily physical pain and tremendous crippling fatigue at times, poor short-term memory, as well as being unable to account for the many memory-gaps of my past and still, at times, irregular sleep-patterns, it's clear to me now that taking care of myself has to be my number-one priority. I'm referring to specifically the *art* of pacing oneself, proper diet, regular physical activity, accountability to yourself and those you love and the constant nurturing of your life as a whole, is required on a regular, daily basis. All of that provides the foundation for one to be able to experience their life as the gift that it is, and not some awful nightmare to be endured, as mine has sometimes looked and felt, to me.

As I wrote in the introduction that this book was nothing short of a monumental effort but I did it. It wasn't *just* me though, as I had the support of those around me too. Yes, I have written very word, no ghostwriter here, although that's a realistic alternative one could consider.

My point is that we will continue to heal for as long as we believe healing is possible. Just keep believing!

And remember:

Nothing of value can really be accomplished in life without the love and support of others.

PHOTOS

A scene from my former water-front home, my rental-house boat located just to the right but nearly fully obscured in this photo. I lived here for a short time before and then for a while after the accident-2001-2003.

My 'New Home' on the water: just a short distance down the dock from my former rental- house-boat, 2006 & 2007 - (the forward bow hatch just visible in the lower right-hand corner of this photo).

Mute Swans and their Cygnets looking for some goodies! At the marina, next to my boat- 2006.

Sammy 1999-2013 (L) & Martin 1998- (R) - a.k.a. The Cats Who Saved My Life! This photo was taken on the balcony of the Heritage Apartment I rented in New Westminster, 2003-2005.

Ten days pre-accident; Waimea Canyon & Fern Grotto, Kauai-
March 2002

Four or Five weeks post-accident -one of 'The Walking-
Wounded,' Vancouver, BC.

More Photos:
https://www.facebook.com/pages/The-Distracted-
Yogi/359538544159483

SOME FINAL THOUGHTS ON MY PERSONAL VIEWS ON BRAIN INJURY RECOVERY

When I was new to the brain injury world, I often heard from specialists and others, (who'd probably heard about it or read about it in what was by then out-dated 'factual' sources) that the healing expectancy for brain injury is generally no more than two years post trauma. It was the same old piece of information regurgitated by experts and legal types throughout much of my recovery but I never believed any of that. I suspected then that the brain was far too tricky a subject to be limited like that. Especially since humans knew much less about their brains, at that time, than we did about most other natural systems of the body or otherwise.

I kept doing the things I'd heard about from close friends who'd read about brain function advancements in health and science periodicals. My friends, it seemed, were more on top of the subject then all the specialists I'd seen. Also, the emerging science regarding the neuroplasticity of the brain has provided all of us with new and exciting angles of truth regarding our brains' ability to heal and physically alter itself.

The point is not to accept something that doesn't feel right to you. You can heal with the right attitude. How to achieve complete healing is still a mystery to me, but I'm certain that if I'd accepted the oft repeated mantra that I was not going to heal beyond the two year mark then, I probably would not have.

My primary message is; accept where you are on any given day as a *temporary* situation, as this will allow your healing to continue, and also, by means of a proper attitude towards the *possibility* of getting better. It will take time, a lot of time, more than you want it to, but that's still okay.

Celebrate your little victories, like remembering something

for the first time then, for the second and the third time too. Every triumph, no matter how insignificant, is important to acknowledge and if you celebrate it you will slowly and eventually create a shift in your awareness of yourself. Each shift in your awareness marks the moment where you've moved forwards in recovery. Rejoice in that success.

I cannot stress enough how important it is to feed your brain. If you are on your own then you are 100% responsible for your own recovery. When we eat poorly, sit around all day watching TV, take up our time and the time of our loved ones with mindless chatter then we are robbing our brains of vital healing energy and nutrition. It's time to get over the idea that good nutrition is too expensive or too time consuming for you. We are talking about your brain here, and if you don't take better care of it then who will? You can take better care of yourself if you make the decision to do so.

Read a little every day. Start with magazine articles, but strictly limit your time on the internet...it can be a rabbit hole! You'll get sucked into the void as hours pass, and you will have gotten out of it only negligible gains to your overall health. Social groups can be great support too, but a few can be self-destructive outlets for our lack of impulse control.

Try learning something new every day. Learning new things can be especially challenging for us, and your frustration levels will peak at times. Take a break from them, then re-commit to more learning the next day.

I tried to learn to play several different musical instruments, and maybe that was always going to end badly, but I still tried and who can really say how much or how little that stimulated the natural healing process of my body, and especially of my brain? I was continually encouraged by my loving and supportive tribe of friends and adopted family to keep challenging myself, but in particular my brain because it actually craves challenge.

Initially, and for a long while after my injury, my vocabulary was almost entirely lost to me, as was my command and comprehension of my first language, English. I lost my former knowledge of French and Spanish, most of which I've not recovered. My trip to Costa Rica was a painful reminder of how far I've yet to go as I stumbled and stuttered my way through the mutual language barriers.

Yes, I'm still a work-in-progress but that's okay because I believe that to some degree everyone is on the same journey in life, whether through trauma or some other live-altering event or situation, we are all in this together.

I don't believe that our recovery has to be limited, especially by our own self-limiting ideas. You will encounter ignorance along the way, but if you address your own fears first, which conspire to keep you in your damaged state, then you too can continue to heal, and in so doing inspire others to do the same.

I wish you well on this journey back to your *new* self.

REFERENCE GUIDE:
HOW-TO TELL YOUR OWN STORY

Many survivors of trauma are compelled at some point in their recovery to write about it or find some medium with which to share their experiences. I encourage you to do the same if you are so inclined to. It took me many years to be able to put this book together, for you and, also for the advancement of my own journey of continued healing. Hiring a ghostwriter is also an option.

The process of publishing a book has been radically simplified due to the tremendous overhauling of the industry. This all coming as opportunity, offered up through the entrepreneurial spirit, which is at the heart of the internet community. E-books now outsell traditional books and can be a great option for you.

Try electronic only options such as Kindle, which is free and provides a generous royalty program through its parent company, Amazon.com, iUniverse is another self-publishing & traditional format publisher, yet a few others are smashwords & createspace and lastly, Balboa, the self-publishing arm of Hay House (Louise Hay) and a host of others. Most offer publishing packages starting at a few hundred dollars (USD), up to many thousands of dollars, depending on your specific preferences.

At the time of writing, these rates, etc. were accurate, however, do your own due diligence. These are your words you're putting out there, so do the proper research first.

Enlist the help of a proper Copy-Editor & Formatting specialist so that your book is more carefully crafted into its greatest potential. Print-on Demand services can be found at: http://www.lulu.com/ & http://www2.xlibris.com/ , to name a few.

For me, my first hope and ultimate goal is to give you something useful, entertaining and timeless. You, the reader will be the ultimate decider of the achievement of these things.

Before embarking on your writing journey, I can offer you several useful bits of information to assist with the process;

- A computer/laptop is a must, loaded with MS Word.

- Download an android app from the 'playstore' called The Pomodoro Method (my personal favorite is Pomodroido). This will assist you with the physical task of disciplined writing (apple will have an equivalent).

- An e-book guide to get you started such as "How to write a non-fiction e-book in 21 days that readers will love!" by Steve Scott. Available through Amazon.com for approximately $5.

- 'Building your book for Kindle', free from amazon.com or pay for some expert formatting.

- Several packages of index cards to build your book in abbreviated form first, something that you will be referring to often to stimulate your memory of specific themes, (re: your injury & recovery) for the proper construction and flow of each chapter you intend to write.

- A 'To Do List' that you must adhere to i.e. Do your writing first thing in the morning, then do everything else after that (*especially* before checking emails and mindlessly surfing the web!).

- Start getting up earlier, if you don't already. You must learn to be more disciplined if you want to make your dream of helping yourself & countless others heal from your personal story of triumph over your brain injury or any other personal trauma.

- You *can* do this but, you will also need something called the *Four Pillars Of Transformation* on your side, they are;

1) **Accountability**- You must be accountable to at least one other person so that you hold yourself, as well as them, to the promise of completing your goal of writing your book.

2) **Achievability**- If you have surrounded and imbibed yourself with the proper knowledge & tools to complete this task then you will succeed. That makes your goal 100% achievable.

3) **Measurable**- You must set defined *end goals* at specific intervals along the way, i.e. if you have determined that your book should be completed within 6 months of starting, (completely doable by the way!) then you must set specific benchmarks along the way. The average e-book is approximately between 200 & 300 pages. This means that if you are aiming for say 250 pages, then you must complete approximately 42 pages per month or 1.5 pages per day. This includes your introduction, thank you page(s), table of contents, references (if any), photos & pictures, bibliography (if any). If you are achieving the goal of 1.5 pages per day, before proofing and editing, then your book is on track!

4) **End time or time limitation**-Your goal to write a book must have a time sensitive value to it. You must set a time limit for its completion or else it, like you, will fall into the vast desert of complacency and self-loathing will reign supreme in your mind! Just do it. Other people need you to as much as you need to do this for yourself.

Get some help from online writer's forums. I joined a contest called 'The Transformation Contest' created by an online newsletter called ETR-Early to Rise. This internet based company runs this contest concurrently throughout the year providing free expert advice along with a closed, contestant community forum. Unlimited access to inspirational articles and practical advice & the genuine support of the contestant forum were by far the biggest contributing factors in my successful writing of this book.

Lastly and most importantly, make it *a good read* or even better make it great! Above all, make it an honest representation of your experience to the absolute best of your knowledge. The truth is powerful enough, so let that be your gift to rest of us!

ODE TO THE (NEWBIE) WRITER-WRITING IS LIKE THE OBSTACLE COURSE IN BASIC TRAINING

Before you write your first book, try comparing the process to going through a kind of military basic training camp.

You start out enthusiastic, but once you've glimpsed the course ahead, your feelings rapidly change into those of dread and insecurity. "I can't do this, can I?!"

Then, you start, looking around for a cue or some clue from the others, and at last, you slowly begin to move through the course laid out in front of you.

Then before you know it, you're down on your hands and knees crawling around in the muck that is your thoughts, "What am I doing here? I'm not even a Writer-am I?!"

Then, you're on your feet again dodging doubt, running ahead, but then once again the path becomes confusing. "Do I jump or wade across the watery chasm that is my story?!"

You eventually take a leap, and now you're feeling fantastic because you know you belong but then, an enormous wall looms just ahead, "Oh God, now what?!"

You grab onto the dangling rope and struggle and struggle to climb up the steep wall that is your nemesis; Doubt and Despair. You continually fall and slip back several notches on the rope, but you keep going because you know the top of the wall is near. You look up thinking you must be there, but it continues to rise high above you, and you feel frustrated and for a moment you consider quitting, packing it in completely. You ask yourself "Why am I even doing this?! "Who would notice if I did, or didn't finish?"

Then it occurs to you, YOU would notice. Now you want to get over that wall just for you, because you must. This was exactly what you needed, a little burst of energy to get you up and over the top, the final obstacle: You Did It!

INTERNET RESOURCES

BRAIN-INJURY ASSOCCIATIONS of BC
& CANADA:
BC: www.bcbraininjuryassociation.com/
CANADA: www.biac-aclc.ca/
BIAC-Bursary Program to pursue education:
www.disabilityawards.ca/details.php?lang=EN&ID=83
Chinese Persons- BI Support:
www.bcbraininjuryassociation.com/resourcePOP.php

HEALTH-GENERAL, BC & CANADA:
BC Healthcare coverage-General Info re: services
www.welcomebc.ca/
Ministry of Health Services: www.gov.bc.ca/health
Child Health BC: www.childhealth.bc.ca
First Nations & Inuit Health Canada: www.hc-sc.gc.ca
Health-Family & Child:
www.canada.com/health/family-child/index.html
CF Family Resources:
www.forces.gc.ca/site/fam/index-eng.asp

VICTIM SERVICES:
Are You Being Abused? British Columbia, Canada- only;
Victimlink-24 hour: 1 800-563-0808, www.bc.ca/cserv

OTHER RESOURCES-
USA, England (UK), Australia, Europe & Others:
USA: www.biausa.org/
UK: www.headway.org.uk/
Acquired BI Forum-London, UK: www.abil.co.uk/links/
AUSTRALIA: www.braininjuryaustralia.org.au/
Support for ABI and Caregivers: www.Heasdwest.asn.au

EUROPE: www.ebisssociety.org/infos-eng.html

For All Other Countries Not Listed:
www.internationalbrain.org

MISCILLENEOUS:
Statistics & Demographics (USA):
www.caregiver.org
CDC (USA):
www.cdc.gov/traumaticbraininjury/pdf/Future_of_Registrie
s-a.pdf

BRAIN HEALTH LINKS:
Brain Games & Brain Training: www.luminosity.com
Neuroplasticity:
www.youtube.com/watch?v=iAzmyB9PFt4
&
www.bigthink.com/think-tank/brain-exercise
&
www.medterms.com/scriptmain/art.asp?articlekey=40362
&
one more-PBS Secret Life of the Brain and Neuroplasticity:
www.sharpbrains.com (search the above title)

ORIGINAL COVER-ART
THE ARTIST'S BIOGRAPHY

Stacy Renee McCusker is an intuitive artist who combines art; healing and energy work into her creations. Stacy has a rich history which includes dance, meditation, art and performance. She works with children and adults in both the meditative and creative arts. She has recently embarked upon a unique style of healing art. She listens to ideas and dreamy descriptions from her clients, and then paints them into reality on canvas. She is blessed by her connection with Michelle, by being troubadours of transformation together. "I am forever grateful for my opportunity to provide Michelle with her cover art, for this most important and needed book."

Stacy is currently working on a transformational calendar that will help infuse 2014 with beauty and healing. Visit her store at http://www.etsy.com/shop/CosmicArts or follow her blog at http://dreamwithstacy.wordpress.com/. Also, please visit her page at Kickstarter and support her desire to bring light and love to all,

http://www.kickstarter.com/projects/126420968/bliss-2014, pledging cycle valid until June 26, 2013.

Take a beautiful step further and dive into the

transformational, healing adventure of your life with her unique style of coaching. Her sessions weave a tapestry of healing for her clients, through life coaching and paintings, that helps bring visual, color and energy upgrades to enhance the transformational experience. Email Stacy at stellarjoycoach@gmail.com for further information.

May the great eastern sun continue to shine upon our soul's mission.

Blessings, Stacy Renee McCusker

ABOUT THE AUTHOR

Michelle G Desgagne has dreamed of writing her first book, the one you are holding in your hands or reading as an eBook, for more than 10 years. It has been a brutal path but she is a Warrior after all! She currently lives, with her cat Martin, in Vernon, British Columbia, Canada.

Her next book is the prequel to The Distraced Yogi and is titled 'The Reluctant Lesbian." It will be completed sometime later this year. Another project which has been inspired by her Vision:'To Uplift Women & Girls so that they may embrace their confidence and self-belief, and then, they too can join in the ongoing co-creation of the reality of a better, loving, supportive & inclusive world-view that we are all so privileged to part of.' 'And, in doing so we will, All of Us, make an enormous contribution to the re-construction of our collective, mental & emotional-world-view. We may even, in the process, alter our Mother-Earths ability to heal herself & so too heal All of Us as well'.

Specifically, Michelle is in the process of creating a series of How-To Guides in traditional, eBook & DVD formats-geared towards the needs of women & girls;
<u>The Women's Illustrated Guide to Power-Tools &</u>

<u>Their Uses:</u>

<u>You Can Do It! & This Guide Will Show You How!</u>

&

<u>The Girls Mini-Guide to Hand Tools & Their Uses</u>

Visit <u>PowerToolRevolution.com</u> soon, to learn more about it or to connect with <u>Michelle's Blog</u> & other useful 'fix-it-chick' links.

<u>http://www.prettyhandygirl.com/</u>

<u>www.jacobeducation.com/HandywomanHomeRepairs.html</u>

<u>http://home-maintenance-for-women.com/</u>

<u>http://voices.yahoo.com/a-womans-guide-home-repair-6225298.html?cat=30</u>

"Of all the things I've lost I miss my MIND the most"
Bumper sticker on my car 1989-1992

19807687R00137

Made in the USA
Charleston, SC
12 June 2013